MW00572127

SNOWMOBILE ADVENTURES

AMAZING STORIES

SNOWMOBILE ADVENTURES

The Incredible Canadian Success Story
from Bombardier to the Villeneuves

SPORT/HISTORY
by Linda Aksomitis

PUBLISHED BY ALTITUDE PUBLISHING CANADA LTD.
1500 Railway Avenue, Canmore, Alberta T1W 1P6
www.altitudepublishing.com
1-800-957-6888

Extreme care has been taken to ensure that all information presented in
this book is accurate and up to date. Neither the author nor the
publisher can be held responsible for any errors.

Publisher	Stephen Hutchings
Associate Publisher	Kara Turner
Editor	Jay Winans
Digital Photo Colouring	Scott Manktelow

We acknowledge the financial support of the Government
of Canada through the Book Publishing Industry Development
Program (BPIDP) for our publishing activities.

Altitude GreenTree Program
Altitude Publishing will plant twice as many trees as were used
in the manufacturing of this product.

National Library of Canada Cataloguing in Publication Data

Aksomitis, Linda
Snowmobile adventures / Linda Aksomitis

(Amazing stories)
Includes bibliographical references.
ISBN 1-55153-954-3

1. Snowmobiling--History. 2. Snowmobiles--History. I. Title. II. Series

GV856.5.A47 2003   796.94   C2003-905913-8

An application for the trademark for Amazing Stories™
has been made and the registered trademark is pending.

Printed and bound in Canada by Friesens
2 4 6 8 9 7 5 3 1

Cover: Jacques Villeneuve racing during the 1987–88 season

I dedicate this book to my indispensable research assistant, Rosemary Daver, and to my grandson, Jonathon Daver-Aksomitis, so that he will be able to read about the great Canadians who contributed so much to the sport of snowmobiling we love as a family.

An early Bombardier snowmobile prototype from the 1950s

Contents

Prologue

In 1960 a little prairie girl started school. Her home was a long way from the highway. In the fall, her father drove her to school every morning in a rickety old truck. When the first snows arrived, he ploughed through them.

Blizzards dumped more snow on the prairie. A lot of it caught in the trees along the trail, which passed for a road. Soon, it was easier for the truck to drive through the field than it was to go down the road.

The little girl loved school. She cried when bad weather kept her at home. She missed her books.

There were no school buses. But there were other parents taking their children to school. The little girl's father contacted a nearby family to make arrangements.

"Can you take her along with your kids?" asked the father.

"Sure," laughed the neighbour. "There's lots of room in the Bombardier."

On Monday morning the little girl waited at the window. She heard it coming. It roared like father's

tractor. But she still couldn't see it through the snowdrifts.
Closer and closer came the roar. She grew nervous.

Finally, its light-coloured body emerged from the snow. Father said, "Tie up your scarf and hurry outside. I'll come with you."

She followed father out of the house. The smell of exhaust was strong. Closer and closer she walked toward the rumbling machine. She dodged the two big skis at the front.

The door fell open before father could touch the handle. The neighbour smiled. "Good morning. So you're ready for school?"

The little girl nodded. She peered around the inside of the machine. The neighbour sat in the big front seat, his hand on the gear shifter. His heavy winter parka was partly unzipped. Behind him, the children sat on benches, snug in their coats and mittens.

Father helped her into the Bombardier. She wanted to say no, I'd rather stay home. But, the words caught in her throat. The fearful machine was the only way to get to school.

Hurrying, she sat down beside the only other girl. "Hello," she yelled, over the engine's roar.

The older girl moved over to make room on the wooden bench. "Hang on to your books or they'll fly away," she warned.

Prologue

The Bombardier door closed. The little girl saw father wave through the big front window. Then the machine started to move. Loose items slid across the floor. The boys laughed.

Slowly the Bombardier began to make its way over the snow. Through the window the girl saw a large snowdrift ahead. She was scared! She braced her feet. Things slid everywhere. She hung on. Up went the Bombardier. Down went the Bombardier. Then it came to another bank. Up and down it went again.

"This is fun," she said. The boys grinned. The older sister grimaced, clutching her books.

That little girl was me. I'd bought into Bombardier's dream of travelling over the snow.

Chapter 1
J.-Armand Bombardier's Dream

In the early days of the 20th century, as a distant war raged in Europe, a group of boys in Quebec piled onto their toboggans as the snow flew around them. They sped down the hill and tumbled out when they reached the bottom, shrieking with laughter. Joseph-Armand Bombardier grabbed the rope on his sled to pull it up the hill again. With each step, his legs sunk into the snow to the depth of his knees. The ride down the hill was brief and exhilarating, the climb up difficult and tiring. Young J.-Armand dreamed of a machine he'd invent some day — a machine that would glide over the snow and maybe even *climb* the snow-covered hills of Quebec, pulling his toboggan easily to the top for him.

In 1907, when J.-Armand Bombardier was born near Valcourt, Quebec, snowshoes were the only way to float over the snow. Every other method of transportation sunk into the snow, leaving deep tracks. Today, Canadians *skidoo* across the snow with his Bombardier snowmobiles. Over the years other French Canadians also participated in the development of the snowmobile. This book tells their amazing stories.

J.-Armand's first snow machine
From a very young age, J.-Armand was a mechanical genius, as though he was born with a wrench in his hand. The Bombardier family lived on a farm, a great place to develop mechanical talents. As the oldest son, he had lots of opportunity to get his hands greasy fixing things around the farm, even things his father and uncles had abandoned as completely worn out.

His father, Alfred Bombardier, moved the family into the town of Valcourt when J.-Armand was 13 years old to open a general store. J.-Armand no longer had the farm equipment to work on, but he turned his attention to building models and toys for his nine younger siblings. Once he made a working tractor out of old clock parts. Later, he invented a method to operate his aunt's spinning wheel using steam power. For that project he used parts from an old tire pump, along with tubes, a valve, and a crankshaft.

But by his teens, J.-Armand, like many boys, wanted larger projects to work on. He was especially fascinated with cars. He even took the family car apart on occasion to see how it worked.

Alfred Bombardier needed to find some way to satisfy his son's interests without sacrificing the family vehicle, so sometime during the winter of 1922–23, he found an old Model T Ford. The salesman assured him that the car was beyond repair, so Alfred purchased it to keep 15-year-old J.-Armand busy.

J.-Armand and his younger brother, Léopold, spent all of their Christmas vacation working on the car. They tightened bolts. They removed parts. They adjusted settings. But, as always, it was the motor J.-Armand was most interested in. The Model T's body and frame offered a curious and mechanical mind many hours of entertainment, but more than anything else he wanted to hear the engine run.

The holidays passed quickly. On New Year's Eve, 1922, the town of Valcourt was covered with a crisp new blanket of white snow. Horses were tied to the hitching posts, and people chatted in the streets, celebrating the last day of the year. A few cars rumbled along, leaving tire trails over the sleigh tracks. Little did the townspeople know, history was about to be made in Valcourt. J.-Armand opened the door of the family's garage. A grin spread across his face as he and Léopold pushed their invention onto the street that ran through their quiet neighbourhood.

The machine machine elements from both a sleigh and a car. It had a metal framework that joined long rear sleigh runners and shorter front runners without any of the more obvious amenities, such as long seats or a deck. The Model T engine, which was never supposed to run again, was securely mounted in the middle of the framework. A shaft connected the engine to a large propeller at the rear of the machine — the propeller would help drive the machine forward over the snow.

J.-Armand needed to crank his engine to start it — the modern ignition system was still a future invention. He and his brother shared their duties: J.-Armand, the mechanic, took the engine controls, ready to bring his creation to life; Léopold was at the other end, steering. Their horseless sleigh was ready for its trial run.

The engine revved up, roaring loudly enough to bring their father to his feet inside the family home. Rushing to the window, he watched as his two sons glided out of the yard perched upon an incomprehensible contraption with flames belching out of the direct exhaust manifold. Alfred was horrified!

Léopold used his feet to steer the machine out onto the street, pushing the front skis in the direction he wanted to turn. The method lacked precision, but it was sufficient to keep the motorized sled from running into anything.

Propellers whirling around, the sled picked up speed and the boys were soon sailing down the street. Startled children screamed and animals scurried to escape the machine hurtling toward them. Women shook their heads and lamented the troubles endured by the Bombardier boys' poor mother.

J.-Armand drove proudly down his hometown's street for more than a kilometre. Behind him ran Alfred Bombardier, waving his arms and shouting.

When, breathless, Alfred finally caught up to his sons, he ordered them home immediately with the contraption. Once there, he made sure they dismantled it before it could cause someone an injury.

J.-Armand Bombardier had made his first drive with a snow machine — his life had its purpose.

But did J.-Armand invent the snowmobile on that historic day, as many people believe? There has always been controversy around exactly who invented the snowmobile — with most Canadians believing it was J.-Armand. But J.-Armand Bombardier wasn't the first or only inventor determined to find a way to travel over the snow.

Starting in 1913, Virgil White built and sold car-snowmobile conversions in New Hampshire. These consisted of a track and ski unit for the Model T Ford, and later, the Model A. In fact, White applied for a patent on his machine, which was granted using the name *snowmobile* long before J.-Armand's drive. In Saskatchewan, when a snow machine is registered to get license plates, it isn't called a snowmobile at all, but rather a *motor toboggan*. The reason for this can be traced to Carl Eliason, from Saynor, Wisconsin, who invented a small, single-person snow machine using a toboggan and a boat motor, which he patented as the *motor toboggan* in 1927. The snow machine we ride today is based more on Eliason's patent than on White's or even J.-Armand's first invention, despite the confusion over the names. J.-Armand did invent and patent many things that certainly revolutionized the industry, but snow machines were patented in the U.S. before J.-Armand began serious work in the area.

Father and Inventor
J.-Armand was the quintessential preoccupied inventor. He worked from sunup until sundown, 12 or 14 hours a day. Always interested in why things worked and how to

make them better, his mind was distracted by interesting ideas for machines and inventions, leaving little room for conversation or even polite exchanges with people. Indeed, with grease-stained overalls and permanently dark hands from working with engines and metal, he seemed to have no social graces at all, sometimes interrupting activities or conversations when a new thought occurred to him.

J.-Armand was a family man, too. On August 7, 1929, he married Yvonne Labrecque. During the next 15 years they had six children: Yvon, Germain, André, Hugette, Claire, and Janine. J.-Armand opened his own business to support his family: Garage Bombardier. His community, especially his church, also benefited from his energy and commitments.

Winters in the Eastern townships of Quebec were long, while the days were short. Farmers didn't bring J.-Armand as much work to do, so he had more time to work on his dream of travelling over the snow by machine. He experimented with different prototypes, even selling a few to local businessmen. Some were car-conversion snowmobiles, similar to those built and sold by Virgil White. Some were single-seater machines. And some were even propeller-concept snow machines, based on the dismantled snow machine of his childhood. However, by the mid-1930s he was still not

J.-Armand Bombardier photographed in 1942

satisfied with the progress he'd made. It was very simple
— J.-Armand didn't want to plough or drive through the
snow; he wanted to float on top of it.

In the winter of 1934, J.-Armand had sold all of the
snow machines he'd built and was still mulling over the

changes he'd like to make before building the next one.

One snowy day, his son, Yvon, developed a serious fever. J.-Armand and Yvonne tried the usual things to help little two-year-old Yvon, but the child continued to cry, growing hotter and weaker as the hours passed.

Taking his turn rocking the baby, J.-Armand wished he had a snow machine working. Then, he could take little Yvon to a doctor, or bring one to him, instead of listening to him suffer.

The hours passed. Yvon grew worse. The nearest hospital was nearly 50 kilometres away, but it might as well have been a thousand, since the roads were all blocked with snow.

Eventually, the child died of an acute attack of appendicitis. J.-Armand promised himself that he would change the future of rural communities like Valcourt. They needed a dependable way to beat winter conditions so they could access medical help and other necessities. J.-Armand knew his dream was important not just to him but also to others who lived in snowbound areas.

J.-Armand Bombardier's Sprocket
J.-Armand set seriously to work to solve the dilemma of winter transportation. In 1937, he was granted a patent for the B7 *snowmobile*, which, along with the models

J.-Armand Bombardier's Dream

that came after it, became much more widely known as the *Bombardier* (pronounced bom-ba-deer). It included the most revolutionary of his inventions: the sprocket. His sprocket was a simple design consisting of a small wheel with teeth protruding from the external edge of a circle. The teeth weren't sharp; instead they were human-like, wide and flattened at the top. Today, this sprocket is the Bombardier trademark symbol used on products manufactured all over the world.

J.-Armand had been thinking about his problem for three years. All of the machines he built were heavy and ploughed through the snow, having no shock absorption. Then he hit upon a solution — a rubber-encased sprocket with a rubber-belt track. This innovative design propelled his snow machine reliably over the snow instead of through it.

Driven by his desire to make rural areas safe, mobile, and accessible, J.-Armand's efforts weren't concentrated on individual snow machines, but on ones that could transport several people safely over snowy terrain. His B7 snowmobile was large enough to carry seven passengers. It featured some of his best inventions, including a revolutionary rear-wheel drive and suspension system. J.-Armand was satisfied with the design of the B7 and so were his customers. Over the next five years his company produced and sold a total of 150 of the new snowmobiles.

The B7 was a remarkable machine. While the prototype still used a Ford chassis and a few Ford body
parts, the engine was located in the rear, with the hood
facing backward. People couldn't tell which way it faced.
In fact, a police officer once nearly gave J.-Armand a
parking ticket for being in the space backward.

Each season J.-Armand improved the machines
and built up his fledgling company, while running his
general repair shop. Soon, the B7 no longer looked like a
Ford car — it acquired a rounder shape covered with
plywood on the outside. It had lots of room for passengers. A small number of rural doctors, hunters, mission-
aries, even travelling salesmen and taxi drivers began to
use the snowmobile — not a booming customer base,
but a sufficient number of interested folks to justify
staying in business from year to year in those early days.

The drive train was also modified: J.-Armand
improved the rear suspension, and parallel bars sup-
ported the rear wheels, which were linked to the body
with leaf springs. A rubber track looped over the wheels,
connecting with the innovative drive sprockets. At the
front there were still two skis, which the driver con-
trolled with his steering wheel from inside the B7.

J.-Armand wasn't drawn to inventing to become
wealthy — he dreamed of improving the quality of life of

his family, his friends and neighbours, and his province. Like the child who had powered his aunt's spinning wheel with steam, J.-Armand, the adult, wanted to build things that would help other people. He approached inventing by asking what people needed. Nevertheless, J.-Armand was soon making a good income selling snowmobiles and was finally able to leave the repair business for things that interested him more. He renamed his business L'Auto-Neige Bombardier. Always committed to family, he brought in his extended family as employees: four brothers and three cousins.

Unlike the assembly lines of later production in the Bombardier Company, in the beginning each snowmobile was hand built. J.-Armand made sure each hole was drilled correctly, each weld strong. The employees took every question and problem to J.-Armand, the shop foreman, the expert. There was, no doubt, a well-worn path from the shop floor to his office.

The snowmobile business grew one snowmobile at a time. J.-Armand approached his business the same way he approached inventing — with dedication and creativity. He had a single-minded purpose: to deliver his snowmobile to all of those who would find it valuable. By inventing the machine of his boyhood dreams, he had accomplished more than most men do in a lifetime, but the greater challenge of marketing and sell-ing the snowmobile lay ahead. Would enough people want it?

Chapter 2
Building the Dream

oseph-Armand Bombardier nurtured his business with a keen sense of vision and entrepreneurial skill. In the beginning he handled every aspect of the business, including his own marketing. He was sure that seeing was believing, so he took his machine around the province of Quebec, demonstrating it wherever he could.

Selling the Bombardier Snowmobile

Starting in Quebec's small towns, J.-Armand enjoyed surprising people with his snowmobile's abilities. He took the editor of the local newspaper for a ride and let him feel the way the machine rode up over snowdrifts, scooting across the snow-covered terrain. His time always paid off in front-page stories by reporters who were impressed with the modern technology and the young inventor.

J.-Armand didn't stop with the small towns. The snowmobile roared into old Quebec, past the stone walls of the original fortification, which had been built to protect it from invasion from the St. Lawrence Seaway below and the land mass around it. Grey bricks of assorted shapes and sizes, all mortared firmly together to create impenetrable walls, should have provided enough of a barrier to intimidate such machines as J.-Armand's from passing under. But they didn't.

That day, people tramping through the snow watched in amazement as the snow machine crawled toward the city.

It was, of course, winter. Snow shrouded the city, covering its stone and brick buildings, its cobblestone streets.

Le Chateau Frontenac, an impressive structure that seemed to be more castle than hotel, reigned majestically over Old Quebec from its perch on top of the Cap Diamont Cliffs. Its European style complemented the city, its centuries of history, and its friendly people.

From the cliffs the city dropped down to the St. Lawrence Seaway. A few ships sat in dock, echoing with the sounds of the carpenter's hammer where winter repairs were underway. A lengthy toboggan slide ran from near Le Chateau down the hill. Children regularly enjoyed one of winter's best sports as they laughed and shouted, pushing each other down the slide. The air was crisp, below freezing, and their breath came in puffs.

J.-Armand drove his B7 snowmobile down the street; the machine purring contentedly and belching out clouds of exhaust. Shoppers, storekeepers, visitors, and local people all stopped to stare in amazement.

But J.-Armand wasn't content with merely showing Quebecois that his snowmobile could travel easily over the snow. He needed to prove that it could do anything.

He focused on the toboggan slide, inching his machine toward it.

Children stopped, their mouths wide open in amazement. They scurried away from the hill as the mechanical beast approached. J.-Armand, with all of the confidence of a proud inventor, turned his snowmobile around at the foot of the hill.

Spectators wondered what he would do and whether his amazing machine could climb a hill. But J.-Armand was not only sure his snowmobile *would* climb up the hill, he was sure it would do it in reverse!

Twirling the snowmobile around to demonstrate

how manoeuvrable it was, J.-Armand attempted one of his most daring escapades.

He looked up at the toboggan slide, calculating his chances. It was a gamble, but worth it. Taking a deep breath, he revved the engine of the B7.

The snowmobile started its ascent up the hill.

Chugging like the workhorse it was, the B7 backed up the lengthy toboggan slide as spectators watched, their mouths open in amazement. It was, for J.-Armand, a giant publicity coup that proved his confidence in the B7 snowmobile was well placed.

New Markets, New Inventions

For the company, the demonstration translated to more sales and a wider marketplace. With the great performance of the new snowmobile, J.-Armand and his company survived the Great Depression of the 1930s without any difficulty. By 1940, he'd built a new factory to produce 200 snowmobiles annually. But if the Depression didn't have the power to halt Bombardier's growth, the war did. The War Measures Act, which focused all of Canada's economy and production on the war, hit the company hard. New purchasers had to prove that the machine was essential to their livelihood, which, if they hadn't been using it, was difficult to do.

So, J.-Armand turned his inventive talents toward a

machine that would be beneficial for the war effort. The B1 was a military snowmobile prototype, which included numerous innovations patented in both the U.S. and Canada. By 1942, J.-Armand's move into big business required company changes again. He incorporated his company, naming it L'Auto-Neige Bombardier Limitée.

In May 1943, J.-Armand completed the Mark 1, an all-terrain vehicle with a 150-horsepower Cadillac engine. The Mark 1 was the first in a series of armoured snowmobiles, followed by the Mark 2 and the Mark 3, also known as the Penguin. The long vehicle had a full track under it that enabled it to crawl through all kinds of terrain, from snow to swamps. A few thousand machines based on J.-Armand's designs were manufactured, although other manufacturers produced most of those purchased for the military. As a result of the war years, future Bombardier machines incorporated four important patented innovations: wheel mounting, the traction device, the vehicle spring suspension, and the rubberized sprocket wheel.

However, even at the end of the war, it wasn't clear sailing for the young corporation. The Canadian government implemented a new tax, the excess profits tax. The tax limited profits to 50 per cent of the average profit made during the four years preceding the war and was intended to prevent manufacturers from profiting on the unique business opportunities created during wartime. Of course, those years had preceded Bombardier's huge expansion and investment, so the tax was disastrous. Eventually J.-Armand convinced the government to look at his case on an individual basis, and he was finally able to achieve a more realistic deal. The government also refused to pay J.-Armand what he felt was a fair royalty on their use of his inventions for machines they had built. Instead, they offered him a miniscule amount that insulted him. In the end he dropped negotiations and received nothing.

Always moving forward, J.-Armand's next invention, in 1953, was the Muskeg, an all-track vehicle used in logging and exploration around the world. Purchasers of the Muskeg used the machine for such varied and innovative purposes as clearing sand dunes in the Sahara Desert and hauling skiers uphill. J.-Armand also produced other pieces of equipment that revolutionized the logging industry, such as the Bombardier Processing Unit and the Red Ram.

Around the world, the fledgling movement toward providing easy, economical transportation over the snow had already begun. In 1955, in Minnesota, Polaris Industries began manufacturing snowmobiles in a small plant. They sold a single-seat model called a Sno-Traveler. Edgar Hetteen took his Sno-Traveler to

The Pas, Manitoba in 1957 and organized a race between a team of dogs and a snowmobile at the Trapper's Festival. The snowmobiles beat the dogs, but it was a very close race. However, people in the North were impressed, which resulted in Polaris receiving a contract to deliver 25 Sno-Travelers to a dealer in Winnipeg. Mike Bosak, of Beausejour, Manitoba, also built snow machines. From 1950 on, he sold about 50 Bosak Power Toboggans a year in his area.

J.-Armand's Miniature Snowmobile

J.-Armand's business was running smoothly again by 1957, so he had time to return to his boyhood dream of floating over the snow on a small snowmobile. His seven-passenger B7 Bombardier snowmobile had been selling for two decades. The sprocket had made a large impact on the world, and he had dozens of other patents to incorporate into his miniature snowmobile.

J.-Armand was a perfectionist. He wanted to develop a truly functional small snowmobile, unlike early machines he'd built, which he felt were too complicated for mass production. In 1957, he finally built a new prototype that was close to what he wanted.

The prototype resembled an old-fashioned bathtub with its protruding front and high sides. The driver, with only his head sticking out of the machine, could have been sitting in an armoured car, zipping over the snow almost completely enclosed. In fact the sides came up almost to his armpits. Riding in it was like sitting in a tin boiler used to heat wash water on a woodburning stove.

But other than its odd looks, which were changed with the second prototype, there was one significant improvement over the design other snowmobiles of its era. It had the engine in the front of the sled, with an all-rubber track completely beneath the driver's seat. Although the first Eliason motor toboggans used front engines, they didn't in 1957. The Eliason, along with other models of snowmobiles at that time, used rear-mounted engines. These innovations, along with the fact that J.-Armand was the first to mass-produce snow machines (rather like Ford with the motor car), secured J.-Armand Bombardier's reputation as the inventor of the snowmobile.

The new geometry of the sled changed the way the machine handled and rode, making it more manoeuvrable. J.-Armand's many years of experience with the rubber tracks and the rubber sprocket of the B7 and later snowmobiles gave him a big advantage over his competitors. His new, small snow machine was a giant leap ahead of the competition.

But J.-Armand wasn't the kind of inventor who

rushed into production hoping for the best. Before he put his little snowmobile on the market, he wanted to be sure it measured up to his high standards. The next winter, after frequent trial runs, he made more changes.

First he removed the sides, leaving the machine with a front hood that was almost triangular, folded over the engine. Unlike modern snowmobiles that are generally wide and close to the ground, the early snowmobiles were higher and narrower. The hood was a big round bubble covering a lot of empty space — after all, the engines were small and there were no exhaust pipes.

The suspension, tracks, and design that J.-Armand adapted from the big snowmobiles were working just as he dreamed they would. The engine, a four-speed Kohler, which propelled the sled at 15 miles (24 km) per hour over the snow, was satisfactory. He made a few other changes in set-up and had the first hood painted yellow, a colour that stood out in the snow. The top line of detailing, of course, said "Bombardier's," while the second line was painted into a diamond-shape that read "Ski-Dog."

But the name "Ski-Dog" didn't last. Squeezed into the corner of the diamond, the "g" appeared as an "o" and was often misread. Thus, the "Ski-Doo" was born. J.-Armand approved the change, which made sense, as it was easier to pronounce in both French and English.

But there was still one important detail to address before the company would begin production of the Ski-Doo — market testing. Not satisfied with just doing his own test runs, J.-Armand took the machine to the North where he felt it was really needed.

On April 19, 1959, J.-Armand visited the Ojibwa people at Lansdowne House in North Ontario. The little machine was in his Norseman plane.

Lansdowne House, situated on the 55th parallel, had already been the destination of a tractor train used by the Army to study the viability of the Mid-Canada line, which was an air defence early warning line that became operational in January 1958. The people were familiar with technology and keen to try the latest invention when J.-Armand unloaded it from his airplane.

Reverend Fr. Maurice Ouimet, O.M.I. at Lansdowne House, greeted his old friend, J.-Armand, at the landing strip. He was, no doubt, excited when he saw the new machine being unloaded from the plane.

Local residents, even more curious, clustered around the Ski-Dog, as it still was called.

J.-Armand, always keen to show people how he could help them, explained how the Ski-Dog worked. Of course the local men were keen to go. By mid-April it was only two months until the summer solstice when the area would have close to 20 hours of light during the day, so there was lots of time to take test runs.

The dogs watched as the snowmobile roared through the community. So did J.-Armand. He didn't want the trappers to baby his invention. He wanted them to ride as hard as they would while tending their trap lines. He encouraged them to ride it in as many different conditions and through as many different terrains as they could find.

Undoubtedly, the Northerners raced up and down over the snow and ice, jumping over hardened banks and zipping around obstacles. For three full days they rode, filled it with fuel, then rode some more.

When the test run ended, J.-Armand loaded up the Ski-Dog in his airplane. He was very close to being satisfied. With a few more small improvements his little snow machine would be ready to sell to the general public.

With final improvements made, the Ski-Doo went on sale in the fall of 1959. It was the first snowmobile to be mass-produced, with 225 units manufactured in the plant that year. People loved the sleek design of the little yellow machine. Other snowmobiles were large and unwieldy, but J.-Armand's little machine floated over the snow.

In his letter to prospective snowmobile dealers, J.-Armand called his machine a motorized snow-scooter named Ski-Doo. The machine was light and fit

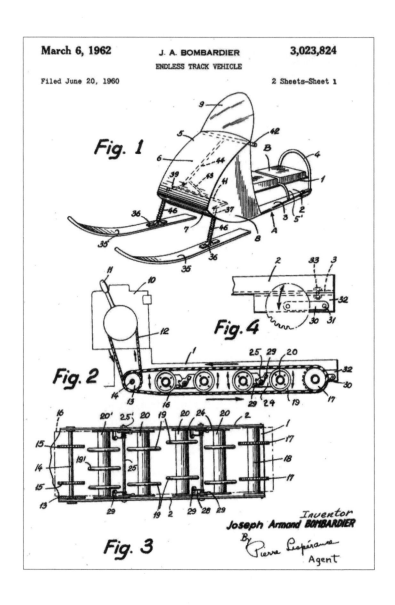

March 6, 1962   J. A. BOMBARDIER   3,023,824

ENDLESS TRACK VEHICLE

Filed June 20, 1960   2 Sheets—Sheet 1

Fig. 1

Fig. 2

Fig. 4

Fig. 3

Inventor

Joseph Armand BOMBARDIER

By Pierre Lesperance

Agent

easily into the box of a 1950s truck, so it was easy for people to load up and haul around. J.-Armand added a postscript to his sales letter saying that he'd heard that Santa sold his reindeers since the Ski-Doo was introduced.

A comparison of the original Ski-Doo to a 2002 Ski-Doo MXZ trail machine shows the differences that more than 40 years of manufacturing have brought to the invention.

	1959 Ski-Doo	2002 MXZ Ski-Doo
Weight	135 kg	209 kg
Overall length	269 cm	275 cm
Overall width	84 cm	115 cm
Overall height	106.5 cm	92 cm
Skis	Wood	Plastic
Max. speed	40 km	125+ km

The company was able to patent his new designs in Canada in 1960. These included an all-rubber endless track, a one-piece chassis, and the use of a manual transmission with a centrifugal variable pulley. In 1962 J.-Armand was also granted a U.S. patent. Unfortunately, many of J.-Armand's earlier design patents had already expired, which made it legal for others to use his ideas.

J.-Armand believed that his inventions could always be improved. In the second year of production, he made several improvements to the Ski-Doo. The first, and most noticeable, was a windshield. The second was a variable-speed v-belt transmission. The third was the addition of coil compression springs on the ski pedestals.

While J.-Armand was generally happy with his little machine that floated over the snow, he wasn't thrilled with the engine. Even though the Kohler was functional, it could be better. Ironically, some of the first snowmobiles had four-stroke engines, like the early Ski-Doo, a trend to which manufacturers in 2003 are returning. The four-stroke Kohler, however, didn't have everything the inventor wanted. Rejecting an engine of his own design, he decided to try a new engine.

J.-Armand found the Rotax engine in Austria. Originally a German company, the Rotax-Werk Ag Company that manufactured the Rotax moved to Gunskerchen in 1947. It gained its popularity as a small engine in the legendary Austrian Lohner scooter, which was how J.-Armand heard about it. Discovering the Rotax was for J.-Armand another part of the dream come true. With the switch to Rotax, Ski-Doos used a two-cycle, instead of a four-cycle, engine.

The Ski-Doo models sold in the 1962–63 season

A B12 model snowmobile

had numerous improvements. The engine purring under the hood was the Rotax, offered in three different engine sizes. The hood itself was made of fibreglass, an easy and economical material to repair. This was important to the ever-growing numbers of snowmobile drivers, since cracked hoods from running into tree branches and other hazards were an ongoing problem.

The modern snowmobiler in late 1962 likely wore a heavy parka, wool pants or layers of jeans and heavy underwear, along with high boots to keep warm. Headgear had to be warm, so toques, or as they are known in some parts of Canada, stocking caps, started to gain importance. Fur hats with ear flaps also made bold fashion statements in some snowmobile circles. Many wore scarves wrapped around their necks, although it soon became evident that this was a dangerous piece of clothing as it was easily caught in the snowmobile's moving parts.

Many snowmobile-related industries started to evolve by 1962, with trailers, sleighs or tag-alongs, and saddlebags the first to gain popularity. From their first season, Bombardier led the industry, becoming the number-one producer of snowmobiles for more than three decades.

J.-Armand Bombardier died on February 18, 1964, at the age of 56. He left behind a thriving corporation that his family developed in the years to follow, first with the snowmobile line and related products, then with numerous other vehicles and products in other industries. J.-Armand's invention exceeded his vision. His humble machine offered to do much more than transport the people of rural Quebec during winter emergencies. The snowmobile was about to take the world on a real adventure.

Chapter 3
The New Era

Snowmobiling appealed to adventurers. It was an outdoor experience that let people access previously unreachable terrain with ease. Bombardier's advertising campaign focused on this type of buyer, promising new thrills in winter sports with the purchase of a Ski-Doo snowmobile. To make the snowmobile even more enticing for winter lovers, Edgar Hetteen, of Polaris Industries in Minnesota, made a 1,920-kilometre trip across Alaska in 1960 in just 11 days. His team included two other men and a woman, riding three Polaris Sno-Travelers. But Ski-Doo took on an even greater challenge — the North Pole.

The North Pole
The Plaisted Polar Expedition, sponsored by Bombardier, made its first try for the North Pole in 1967. However, the trip ultimately failed, despite making it to 83 degrees 50 minutes north, or roughly 685 kilometres from the Pole.

Ralph Plaisted was an adventure-loving insurance salesman from White Bear Lake, Minnesota. He saw his first snowmobile in 1964 and immediately bought the machine. Unlike many others, such as trappers or hunters, Ralph was drawn to the machine simply for what it was.

He was determined to prove the usefulness of the snowmobile to everyone who enjoyed winter. In 1965 he made a non-stop trip from Ely to St. Paul, Minnesota, a distance of around 320 kilometres. It took him 13 hours and 52 minutes. With temperatures at –41 degrees Centigrade, he'd proven that snowmobiles could conquer winter, setting a time and distance record for snow travel.

A year later, Plaisted was sitting with friends in Duluth's Pickwick Hotel. They were talking, as usual, about the wonderful new snowmobiles. After setting one record, Plaisted was keen to take on another challenge. Hetteen had already done Alaska, so what was left?

Someone suggested, no doubt joking, that he tackle the North Pole. Much to everyone's surprise, Plaisted jumped on the idea — he had a new vision and mission.

The dream took shape. When a seven-day blizzard halted his first expedition a short distance from the North Pole, he didn't give up. He already had permission from the Canadian government, along with sponsorship from Ski-Doo. He even had an explorer's license he'd worked 15 months to earn. Re-evaluating, Plaisted decided to start a new trip from a different location on the edge of the Arctic Ocean.

First he raised the funds he needed for a second try at the Pole. Then he gathered another team together: Gerry Pitzl was the navigator, Walt Pederson the mechanical engineer, and Jean-Luc Bombardier, J.-Armand Bombardier's nephew, the technician and scout.

Jean-Luc Bombardier also had a dream to conquer the North Pole. The whole family had many close ties, so this Bombardier was thrilled to be able to ride his uncle's great little machine on such a daring adventure. Plus, as the only Canadian, Jean-Luc's experience with Canadian winters in Quebec was a great asset to the team.

The Plaisted expedition was supplied with four new snowmobiles from Bombardier Limitée — SUPER Olympic 300cc models. Three modifications to these machines made them suitable for polar travel. First, a gas reservoir on the hood was perched in a metal holder over the headlight. Second, a shorter seat allowed more storage space. Finally, metal studs in the rubber track increased traction on the ice. The snowmobiles were ready.

On March 7, 1968, the team left with Jean-Luc as the lead driver. They were on Ward Hunt Island in the Baffin area, the last piece of land before the Arctic Ocean. Supplies and fuel would be dropped on the ice as they required them, since they'd have radio contact with U.S. Air Force helicopters.

The trip wasn't easy. Wind blew across the Arctic, hurling snow like a desert sandstorm. When they left it was –51 degrees Centigrade, which is about as cold as it can get. Ice ridges blocked their way, reaching as high as 12 metres, or 40 feet. They encountered breaks in the ice as wide as three metres, or 10 feet. Once, they found themselves perched on floating ice floes. Rushing rivers caused detours that nearly doubled the distance they travelled. Dedication kept the men focused on their goal.

The Ski-Doos ploughed ahead for 1,330 kilometres taking them 43 days, two hours, and 30 minutes. Finally, on April 19, 1968, the team reached the North Pole. Overhead, the U.S. Air Force verified the victory. Jean-Luc Bombardier stood at the top of the world on his Bombardier snowmobile, the one place where every spot of earth was south.

Jean-Luc Bombardier en route to the North Pole in 1968

Plaisted's was the first expedition to the North Pole to be confirmed. Jean-Luc Bombardier was celebrated as the first Canadian to reach the Pole. And Bombardier was justifiably proud of their little machines — Ski-Doo could go anywhere.

The Plaisted Arctic Expedition didn't end when the team reached the North Pole, however; they still had to snowmobile back. It was already past mid-April and spring was coming. The North was full of surprises for the tired explorers. Snow melted, opening the rivers. Several times, they had to rev up their Ski-Doo engines and skip across water. Then winter made a sudden return.

The men huddled on the ice in their tents. Day after day the wind blew. Only their elation at already having made the Pole kept their spirits up.

On the sixth day, the weather cleared. It was nearly May. By June, ships would travel the Arctic Ocean. Every day they spent on the ice was more dangerous. The Ski-Doos set off at a fast pace.

Luckily for the team a ski plane spotted them. Rescue was near. The plane landed and loaded their equipment; however, it didn't have room for all of the Ski-Doos. One had to be left on the ice. It has never been located.

But, even without J.-Armand Bombardier, the Bombardier Company knew how to turn a bad thing into a good thing. That fall, new advertisements showed how the Ski-Doo had crossed the Arctic and reached the North Pole. Their promotion material said, "Somewhere in the middle of the Arctic there is a Ski-Doo parked with the key in the ignition. If you find it, you are welcome to keep it." The story helped make skidoo a household word across Canada.

Reaching the North Pole was one of the key achievements in Jean-Luc Bombardier's life. He died less than two years later, on March 12, 1970, in Valcourt, Quebec.

Snowmobile Racing Begins

It has been said that the first snowmobile race was held the day they made the second snowmobile.

Little races popped up all over Canada in the early 1960s, and a surprising number of spectators showed up to see those crazy snowmobilers run their machines.

The big winners at snowmobile races were the factories. It didn't take long before everybody was chanting the same song: If you could "win on Sunday," you could "sell on Monday." Ski-Doo, like all of the other builders, jumped into racing as the best method of promoting their product and advertising its new features.

Most of the first races were informal challenges on frozen lakes. But as more and more snowmobiles appeared, the competition grew. In 1961 the Hodag Sportsman's Club added a snowmobile event to their ice-fishing derby, which was held at Boom Lake, near Rhinelander, Wisconsin. Five Ski-Doos lined up, with 60-year-old Herman Lassig running away with his 30-mile-per-hour (48-km-per-hour) victory.

The Lions Club at Beausejour, Manitoba, included a snowmobile race in their 1962 annual Winter Farewell festival. Planners hoped that having a power toboggan race would draw bigger crowds, so they laid out a track with bales in a semi-circle on the school grounds, making it snowmobile history's first oval race. Six drivers dared speeds of up to 15 miles (24 km) per hour to determine the winner.

Lac LaRonge, Saskatchewan, also had a race that year. It was a cross-country event over the snow. And, indeed, it was really over the snow, as participants could just see the tips of the evergreen trees through the drifts. According to the rules, drivers couldn't follow anyone else's tracks, so each snowmobile had to break a trail to the two-mile (3.2 km) marker and back again. Pitted against dog teams, the snowmobiles once again proved they could easily out-pull animals over the harsh landscape.

Ski-Doo, with its light weight and better handling, jumped into first place in the marketplace with a lead that was startling even to company owners. Word spread rapidly through race events, so dealers took the little machine to show what it could do.

As 1963 arrived, the snowmobile boom was under-way. During the last weekend of February, 1963, the Beausejour Lions Club in Manitoba held the first formally titled and well-organized race in the sport's history, called the Canadian Power Toboggan Championships. It was essentially the same as their first event but had more competitors and classes.

Over 1,000 people packed the school grounds, peering through their glasses, enjoying the latest competitive sport. With the Bosak Power Toboggan manu-factured right in the area, along with the sales of other brands, snowmobiles were common a sight on Beausejour's streets through the winter.

The day was full of events, so the youngsters were tired enough to stand still and let their parents enjoy the last event of the day.

More or less a circular shape, the track was marked by bales of hay, which even in 2003 are still recognized as the best track liner for driver safety. The first event, a cross-country race, had already been run, and the title awarded. It was time for the Novelty Race of the day, for the ladies.

In the pits, women drivers listened attentively to fathers and husbands giving final instructions. The men told them to keep the engines revved at the starting line so that the machines wouldn't stall; they advised leaning into the turns to avoid crashing into the hay bales on the track's perimeter.

The women handed their scarves to the men in their pit crews and carefully tucked their hair into their hoods.

The men yanked the recoil and the Ski-Doo engines roared to life, two-cycle engines pounding out a steady rhythm of beats only a mechanic could love. Others swore repeated exposure to the sound would make you deaf, if it hadn't already. Four women grabbed the handlebars, claiming ownership, at least momentarily, of the machines. One driver, riding her bright red new Polaris machine, tightened her kerchief around her head. The men, one knee on the seats, manoeuvred their snowmobiles up to the starting line. If the drivers could hear any more of the last-minute instructions over the combined cacophony around them, they ignored them.

The track official lifted the start flag. Children waved at their mothers, aunts, and sisters, dismayed at the lack of response from the women staring intently at the flag. Under the bright afternoon sun, the townspeople of Beausejour grew silent.

The flag dropped.

The racers gunned the sleds and with a tremendous roar headed around the circular racetrack.

Ahead, the first corner loomed. The women glanced at the sleds on either side of them, determined not to let them pull ahead.

They leaned, throwing their heaviest winter pants over the edge of the slippery snowmobile seat, while their lightweight gloves pushed the throttle right to the metal. "Faster!" they yelled, unable to hear their own words over the roar.

Coming out of the corners, the women fought to

straighten out their wildly fishtailing Ski-Doos. They slid back onto their seats, holding the throttle wide open down the straightaway.

Standing aghast in the pits, the men stared at their snowmobiles with fascinated horror. What were those women doing?

As they rounded corner four, one of the sleds threatened to spin out of control. The track officials scurried safely out of the way, while the crowd stepped back too, unable to believe the race in front of them.

The women weren't ladylike at all. In fact, some said they drove like demons. The racetrack encourages an instinct to win, whether it's a novelty race or the feature event, and the women were out to win that day.

The Ski-Doo Racing Team

The 1969–70 racing season was billed as the birth of the honker era. Seven hundred ninety-five-cc three-cylinder engines were on the market, so it was speed or nothing. Factory-sponsored teams roared around racetracks across the country, leading the way on safety and machine improvements.

In Valcourt, Laurent Beaudoin and his team were organizing Bombardier's most intensive racing effort ever. They had a brand new 796cc Rotax ready to drop into the season's best new sleds. Winning on the track would ensure great sales for the new line.

Beaudoin wanted the best drivers for his team, and that didn't just mean drivers who could win. Bombardier liked drivers with flair, in the true French Canadian style — drivers who would stand out in the crowd and make people notice them.

During the summer of 1969, Ski-Doo invited 75 candidates to Valcourt for a racing team trials camp. While it was an unusual time to be driving snowmobiles around, nobody complained.

Ski-Doo put together a team of executives to hand-pick the new team. They asked the drivers questions about themselves and their careers. Nothing missed Ski-Doo's scrutiny, as each prospective driver was screened carefully.

Outside, imagining themselves on a cool winter's day, instead of under a hot summer sun, the men drove the snowmobiles. They raced one another around the dirt test track, while company officials scored the runs, keeping careful track. It was serious business — only the top 18 would make the first eliminations.

The daily regime for each would-be Ski-Doo racer included calisthenics to get in shape, as well as lots of good French Canadian cooking to make sure they were well nourished. Each man needed to be at his best every day.

The New Era

The first round was completed, with 57 of the candidates returning to their everyday lives after having enjoyed a remarkable sporting experience at Ski-Doo's expense. The remaining 18 men began again. Weeks passed as the men worked out and raced, learning lots about Ski-Doo and each other. A 29-year-old motorcycle-racing champion, Yvon DuHamel, emerged at the end of the summer as one of the top eight picks. The last group of 10 were sent home, and the new team started work.

Yvon DuHamel already had a reputation that appealed to Bombardier. He always gave everything he had in a race, with the sole objective of taking home the victory. His bike had been known to end up in pieces on occasion, so it had to be removed by a truck, but everybody who worked with DuHamel knew they had a good chance of being in the winner's circle with him as their driver. That was just the attitude Ski-Doo needed to get to the top of the North American racing effort.

Once the team was picked, preparation began in earnest. Bombardier built the industry's most elaborate race-testing facility, complete with two dyno cells for engine work and a specially surfaced test track with photo timing cells. A huge shop with worktable and tools was provided for each driver far away from the main plant. Top-secret security was maintained at all times.

But that was just the beginning. Since Bombardier had driven up the toboggan hill with his B7 snowmobile, the company knew it was the image of the company and the perception of the potential buyer that was most important. They prepared their drivers carefully for the media — new suits in yellow and black were provided for each driver, along with a hand-painted helmet for safety on the track.

Of course the new 1970 Ski-Doos were the most important part of the package. Each driver received two Blizzard racing sleds, plus his own mechanic. Ski-Doo was serious about winning, so serious that the program would eventually cost Bombardier Ltd. well over one million dollars. Their investment would help create the reputation of a snowmobile legend.

Chapter 4
Yvon DuHamel

von DuHamel was an ordinary kid growing up in Quebec. Like others, he tried smoking a cigarette when he was five, but his mother caught him and warned him that if he smoked he'd stay small and never get tall — but it didn't work that way for Yvon. Even though he never smoked again, he stayed short and wiry, which was one of his biggest advantages on the racetrack.

He liked hockey and played through the different age groups. However, when he entered the Midget league he was still under 100 pounds, while the other players often hit 150. So, although he was fast, he quit and pursued skiing. In his first season on the slopes, he won a trophy there too.

One day, when Yvon was 15 years old, a guy gave him a ride on a motorcycle...

A couple of weeks later Yvon bought his own motorcycle and went to see a motorcycle race. He decided it looked like fun and that he could do it too. Racing whenever he could, he soon built up a reputation and sponsors, so by 1960 he started into the sport on a full-time basis. Between 1963 and 1970, Yvon DuHamel won the Canadian Motorcycle Association's number-one plate seven times.

DuHamel and Ski-Doo

DuHamel's reputation as a hot young motorcycle star was what caught the attention of Ski-Doo. In 1968 they had called the spunky young 28-year-old and offered him a ride, but DuHamel was busy racing motorcycles for Yamaha, so he declined. The next year, Ski-Doo called again, inviting DuHamel to summer camp. Although he had no experience with snowmobiles, he took them up on the offer and went to camp, making it through the trials and on to the winter team.

DuHamel had considerable competition when he hit the snowmobile racetrack late in 1969, considering his snowmobiling to date had been on a dirt track, not snow or ice. Local manufacturer Skiroule, out of

Wickham, Quebec, had a 16-man racing team. Moto-Ski, in La Pocatier, Quebec, was developing a strong line of sleds and drivers. Teams from the United States were also gathering momentum for a big season of winning and selling: Alouette, Rupp, Scorpion, Sno-Jet, AMF Ski-Daddler, along with Arctic and Polaris all had factory-supported drivers.

The industry revved out of control, pushed by the birth of the 795cc high horsepower engines, with Hirth introducing its 793 Hirth Honker to set the pace. Rotax, Sachs, Polaris, Fuji, Kohler, and Kawasaki all jumped on the bandwagon until race rules stopped development at an 800cc limit, but the brute size of the engines paved the way for an eventful season. Factory-directed racing charged full speed ahead.

When the season began in 1969 there were more than 300 events sanctioned by a variety of governing bodies, including the Ontario Snowmobile Racing Federation (OSRF) and Alberta Snowmobile Racing Association (ASRA).

DuHamel's racing career got a slow start in the myriad of races and racers. He pulled into Ironwood, Michigan, ready to show what his Ski-Doo Blizzard could do on the banks of the oval track. But Ski-Doo drove away with nothing when his belt blew in the high horse-powered modified class.

Ski-Doo went back to Valcourt to work frantically on the sleds — they were good, and everyone at Bombardier knew it. The racers were the best. But setbacks kept happening. In Syracuse, New York, DuHamel injured his knees in a mighty high-speed collision in the Empire State Grand Prix, losing the title to teammate Lucien Lamoureux. Things were getting better for Ski-Doo, but not for DuHamel.

Eagle River World Championship Derby 1970
Winning the Eagle River World Championship Derby in Eagle River, Wisconsin, is the peak to which all snowmobile racers and manufacturers aspire. For professional racers, making it through the finals is the dream of a lifetime. One driver, black-flagged in the first corner of the first lap of his qualifying race, was able to hang up his racing boots and declare he'd done what he set out to do after only 15 metres on the Eagle River track. Like climbing one of the world's tallest mountains, just scaling a single peak is a career highpoint. Winning an Eagle is the glorious moment all dream of, although few attain, while a world championship is the ultimate experience.

On January 12, 1970, one of the biggest parties to hit Rhinelander-Eagle River, Wisconsin, started with the fifth Hodag Marathon. It was run, that year, the week before the world championship for the first time. The Sunday afternoon sprint class had the largest field of snowmobiles ever assembled.

Thousands upon thousands of people crammed into every available motel and hotel room within a 100-kilometre radius of Rhinelander-Eagle River. Press — television, radio, magazine, and newspaper writers — scurried around the communities looking for the biggest story. Factory support trailers filled with spare sleds and bins of replacement components lined up in resorts and around the racetracks. It was the ultimate in racing fever.

Yvon DuHamel arrived, feeling that things were finally coming together. His knees were healed, more or less, from his New York crash, and his sled was running flat out. The Hodag was just practice for the world championship, so he had nothing to lose and everything to gain. Qualifying in the marathon for the Hodag Sprints, DuHamel took his first Hodag title, along with Ski-Doo drivers Dan Oberg and Duane Eck.

By the next weekend, the Eagle River World Championship Derby VII attracted nearly 50,000 spectators along with ABC television cameras. Snowmobile racing had made the big time! One of the top moments was when Ski-Doo driver Gaston Ferland set a quarter-mile drag-racing record of 96.55 miles per hour (155.38

km per hour). But the Eagle River Derby has always been about winning a world-championship title on the oval, regardless of the excitement of other events.

Innovations abounded in Eagle River. Tony Fox had his Sno-Pony Sonic Challenger at the Eagle River airstrip to demonstrate its speed and impressive looks. Looking rather like an oversized hot dog, it was long and close the ground. It had an A-frame suspension for the front skis, which was unique on a snow machine at the time. At the rear, on either side of the separate body, were two short tracks in small frames, which allowed the Sno-Pony to glide over the snow. It had a cockpit, more like that of an airplane than a snowmobile, with a flip-up windshield. It was, in that year when men reached for the ultimate speed on snow, one of several specially designed and built machines.

At the racetrack, the Red Nites, a Canadian team promoting their Massey Ferguson snowmobiles, treated thousands of spectators to a performance. Ramp-to-ramp jumping, once a competitive event, had moved to exhibition status.

The gleaming red Massey sleds lined up in the infield of Eagle River, while the crowd roared. The ramps, about almost two metres off the ground at their highest points, were positioned more than a sled's length apart, about a 350-centimetre gap.

Yanking his recoil rope, the first driver brought his engine to life. He waved at the crowd, savouring the cheers and wild abandon of the spectators. It was their energy that fuelled his leap. Straightening his goggles, he made sure the straps were well adjusted over his helmet.

He revved the engine, ensuring it was running smoothly before he started. A cough or sputter from a cold engine could mean he'd drop between the ramps, instead of flying across the open space.

The motor sounded good in his ears. The crowd sounded better.

Settling himself on the seat, the driver grabbed the handlebars of his machine. The windshield was low, almost non-existent, so he had a clear view of the path toward the ramp.

He took a deep breath and stared ahead, beginning his silent countdown. Three...two...one. He hit the trigger.

The Massey shot forward, aimed directly at the wooden ramp. It only took a few seconds to cover the distance. He felt the sled start the climb up the ramp, listening to the noise of the rubber track thudding against the rough surface.

He sat back on the sled so his arms were stretched out in front of him, barely reaching the handlebars, and felt his muscles tense.

The machine lifted and flew.

For less than a second he saw the airspace below him, but it wasn't a snowbank that waited for his landing on the other side — it was the second wooden ramp. Thump! The snowmobile hit and bounced a little before racing down the opposite side.

Once again the crowd roared to celebrate his performance.

In the pits, the professional drivers were preparing for the heats to qualify for the world-championship race. DuHamel wondered if the world-championship title would elude him as it would 99 of the 100 drivers who met in the battle for the nine spots in Sunday's 1970 championship race. Roger Janssen, defending champion of the title, automatically earned the tenth spot in the field.

There was a lot riding on the race — fortunes could literally be made or promising careers lost. Ski-Doo had the most money of the factories at Eagle River invested in their equipment and their team. Yvon DuHamel was the first of what would become a long line of professional race drivers, groomed for the snowmobile racetrack.

The Eagle River track has always been a challenging one. While it is technically an oval, drivers describe it more as two drag strips with short turnouts at the ends. Both corners are tight, with long, wide straight-aways to build up a tremendous amount of speed. The trick at Eagle River is knowing how hot, or fast, you can take your sled into the corners without ending up in the fence. More than one driver has driven straight off the end of the track, seemingly caught in a straight line with a machine devoid of turning ability.

At the end of Saturday's qualifying heat, DuHamel and teammate Duane Eck were both counted among the 10 drivers to run for the Eagle River World Championship title.

In the pits on Sunday, DuHamel prepared for the big race at the Ski-Doo trailer. The machine was running as well as it ever had. The guys at the top expressed their confidence in his win — so much so that DuHamel felt a great deal of pressure. But he thrived on it, after winning seven or eight Canadian motorcycle titles in a row.

Close to 40,000 people lined the high banks along Eagle River's track to watch the championship race start at 3 p.m. Row after row, the earliest arrivals had the most coveted spots right along the start/finish line. At the ends of the tracks, the crowd was only a few people deep, but they would have a close-up view of the crash-es, since the majority happened on the corners.

DuHamel tied his orange USSA bib number 730 over his yellow suit. He yanked on his helmet, making sure the goggles were sitting correctly on top, ready to pull into place at the start line.

Mechanics brought the sleds to life, listening carefully for any odd sounds. At a nod, DuHamel dropped one leg over the seat of his Blizzard and drove it to the edge of the pits, where several other sleds already waited. Overhead the sky was clear, without a sign of clouds. Temperatures were perfect — warm enough for the crowd to enjoy the day, but cool enough for the snowmobiles to run well.

The track official waved the sleds onto the track.

Red Dobbe stood, ready to start the world-championship race.

They say "holeshot," or being first off the starting line, became the word at the line at that race, as the drivers, each highly motivated to win, prepared for the flying start.

Ready...set...go.

Yvon DuHamel took the low line through the first turn and emerged in first place. The track was hard packed, although by the end of the weekend there were some sand and dirt patches showing through. It was, DuHamel learned, a track where no two laps were the same. Each lap the snow had changed or was gone completely, picked up and thrown by the rubber tracks passing over it at whoever was behind.

Yvon DuHamel

Each of the drivers had a line they preferred. Some went high on the bank, almost touching the plywood sheets that lined the track fence to keep spectators off the track. At the end of the corner they could cut down earlier to make it a drag race to the other end. Others took a mid-line, relying on sliding out of the corner, veering toward the outside of the track right alongside the boards, so they didn't have to reduce speed as much in the corners.

With the hum of the engines approaching like a swarm of angry bees, the sleds moved around the track as a single unit until the field began to separate, with the fastest pulling to the front and the others falling further behind.

DuHamel held his Ski-Doo on the tight inside line, taking the shortest and, for him, the fastest, way around the track. He recorded speeds of over 70 miles per hour (113 km per hour) on his Ski-Doo Blizzard. Snow dust swirled behind him — a white wall that blocked his competition, making him the first Canadian to win the coveted Eagle River World Championship title.

Leading the race from start to finish, Yvon DuHamel won the world championship while he was still essentially a rookie. With its January dates and the slow start to the season, he only had around half a dozen races under his belt. While his experience as a motorcycle champion transferred easily to the snowmobile track, he also learned that racing on snow wasn't nearly the same as on other surfaces. Snow is ever changing and always a new experience.

Finishing the First Season

Once the Eagle River Derby ended, manufacturers cut back on racing. After all, how many more snowmobiles could they sell after the end of January? The money would be better spent in the fall, when wins would make sales. Even Ski-Doo reduced its team to half for the remainder of the season. DuHamel, of course, was still in.

DuHamel was on a roll — pumped from his wins and keen to win again. In every race, he stood out in the field of drivers. Newspapers reported his ability to weave through snow dust as if he had a sixth sense. They also watched him closely for photo opportunities, since he could be counted on to make at least one dramatic photo finish at a race. His sled, they said, had just two speeds, full throttle and stopped.

In Malone, New York, DuHamel's 25-lap modified V final was a true showstopper. When the flag dropped, DuHamel and teammate Eck headed into the first corner. The race was on! Flying over the snow on their mighty yellow Blizzards, they were certain crowd pleasers.

But, in line with his reputation, DuHamel's sled blew a belt midway through the race right in front of the grandstand. As the crowd groaned, the field of sleds charged around him. Not to be beaten that easily, DuHamel grabbed his spare belt and ripped open his hood. Like a madman, he yanked the new drive belt into place. Eck passed him — DuHamel was a lap down.

The Blizzard roared to life and DuHamel hammered the trigger. He began a mad chase to gain his position back, charging past slower sleds on the field. Little by little DuHamel got closer to Eck, while the crowd cheered louder and louder.

Once again disaster happened — this time to Eck, not DuHamel. His belt blew in front of the grandstand. Following his teammate's example, Eck replaced his belt and started out again. When the chequered flag fell, DuHamel took first place and Eck came fourth.

The season was a successful one for Ski-Doo, with some impressive victories in place for its first professional factory team. The new Blizzards had done well. In fact, Ski-Doo had its drivers test various experimental parts during the season. What they learned would be incorporated in future consumer snowmobiles.

1970–71 Racing Season
After just a single year of team trials, Ski-Doo abandoned

the format for its 1970–71 racing season. Instead, the company picked the racing team based on such factors as previous performance. Once again, Yvon DuHamel, of course, made the team.

Back in Valcourt, things were busy in the top-secret development areas of the factory. The new racing Blizzards were aluminum based, had slide rails, and new Rotax engines humming under the hoods. Ski-Doo had even built a dragster, the X-4R, which was ready to test. Crackling with the power of four Rotax 776 engines, it sounded like the machine to beat.

Snowmobiles were selling. In 1970, manufacturers had built 480,000 machines. 425,000 sold. In 1971, 565,000 snowmobiles rolled off the line from almost 100 producers — 10 of which were considered major manufacturers. Ski-Doo, promoted by drivers like Yvon DuHamel, had the lion's share of sales.

Money flowed like water. The purses at big races hit at least $20,000 per race, with Beausejour, Manitoba's Canadian Power Toboggan Championships offering $25,000. Lake Tahoe and Detroit, Michigan, offered $50,000-plus each! Five hundred race events were scheduled across every corner of the snow zone. It was rumoured that the Bombardier team's racing budget for the year was $250,000.

Once again, Yvon DuHamel had a slow start to the

Yvon DuHamel

Yvon DuHamel photographed in 1971

season. His first big win didn't come until New Year's weekend in January of 1971, when he drove the improved Blizzard to victory at Syracuse, New York. Less than a week later, the first death in snowmobile racing occurred when a 12-year-old junior, blinded by snow dust, drove off the track and smashed into a tree at Merrill, Wisconsin.

With safety issues at the forefront, drivers at the 1971 Eagle River World Championship Derby were given a choice. Previously, Eagle River had a flying start, but the Lions wanted a standing start for 1971. Drivers were offered a standing start with all 10 sleds lined up, or, two semi-finals with five sleds each, then a world-championship race with only six sleds. The drivers voted to run the full 10-man field.

With record crowds and prize money, the 1971 Derby has been billed as one of the most exciting races ever run. For the first time ever the crowd watched the line-up of 10 face the race director, waiting for the start flag, while heavy snow fell from the sky. It was also the first time that four brands were represented in the field, and fans were geared up to cheer.

Yvon DuHamel, with his Ski-Doo, and Mike Trapp, the hometown boy on a Yamaha, ran a race that kept the crowd in a constant state of anticipation. DuHamel had superior horsepower, but Trapp had better manoeuvrability in his lighter sled. Each lap Trapp closed as DuHamel braked for the turn — sometimes the Yamaha bumped the rear of the Ski-Doo, but DuHamel held his place. Wayne Trapp, Mike's cousin, steadily crept closer to the duelling pair.

By lap 10, the leaders were still ski to ski, diving into the corners like synchronous swimmers. The dance continued, but only one of the men could emerge as world champion. Out came the white flag — one lap remaining. The crowd roared, cheering their champion. Trapp was leading for the third time of the race, and DuHamel was still in second. Holding the throttle wide open, DuHamel roared into corner one on the last lap. He spun out! Before he could straighten out his sled, he gave up second place to Mike Trapp's cousin Wayne. The two little Yamaha 440s with bogey wheels had taken the victory over the sport's fastest 800s.

DuHamel was disappointed at the loss of the world championship. It seemed his season was spiralling downward, especially when Bombardier didn't have the X-4R ready to race for the speed trials scheduled at Boonville in February 1971.

The Boonville Winter Carnival, however, offered an opportunity for DuHamel to get back to the forefront and take home some of the prize money. The USSA had named it the site of its second world series, so it was his second chance.

So far, the season had been frustrating. Just when he could taste victory, his Blizzard would blow a belt. Or, he'd find himself yanking on the starting rope, anxiously waiting to see if the clock ran out on the two minutes allowed once the drivers were called to the start line. If it wasn't one problem, it was another. His patience was pushed to the limit.

DuHamel had already had problems at Boonville the previous year, when Race Director Ed Siebert tossed him out for having track spikes over what the rule book allowed. DuHamel was nervous going in, anxious to avoid any more problems.

The race meet started out well, with DuHamel far out in front during his heat. Then, an accident brought out the red flag — everyone braked to a stop. Once the track was clear again, Siebert, still race director, gave the two-minute line-up call for sleds. But DuHamel's Blizzard wouldn't start.

Yanking at the rope, DuHamel worked on the balking sled. It had to go! A Bombardier mechanic ran out, so Race Director Siebert instantly disqualified DuHamel, even though the mechanic hadn't touched a thing yet. DuHamel exploded, refusing to leave the track. The race director requested that Bombardier officials escort their driver to the pits, but, seeing his temper, they requested a few minutes to let him calm down.

Siebert, determined to run his race, asked New York State Police officers to immediately remove DuHamel. DuHamel's temper really blew! Shoving the race director out of the road, DuHamel fired up his Blizzard, then roared past Siebert, shoving him one more time. Racing toward the pit, he scattered spectators watching the incident.

The state police were in rapid pursuit. Once they got DuHamel off the machine, they escorted him to a New York jail where he was fined $25 for reckless driving by the local law-enforcement agency. The USSA, who had sanctioned the race, however, slapped him with a suspension from all of their events for the remainder of the year and the next racing season. In April, Bombardier's appeal to reduce the suspension until January 1, 1972, was granted. DuHamel was relegated to the races outside the biggest sanctioning body, a major setback in his career, to be sure, but one that would not hold him back from pursing victory.

Chapter 5
Yvon DuHamel
Sets More Records

The 1971–72 racing season didn't get off to a promising start. First of all, Yvon DuHamel was still disqualified from the first races, so his teammate, Gaston Ferland, had to face Ironwood, Michigan, alone with their newly formed Can-Am Snowmobile Racing Team. The team was sponsored by Bombardier but was not a factory team. Other factories, instead of fronting full racing teams, agreed to participate in the Polaris challenge, which included a limited number of races. In an effort to open racing to more drivers, many factories provided contingency money for independents in qualifying races. The Can-Am team fell midway between factory and independent, so they didn't qualify for contingency money or all of the perks they were used to as direct employees of Bombardier.

Promoters weren't happy around the snowbelt either. With less involvement from the factories, there were fewer big names to bring in. They needed big names to draw big crowds — which they needed to provide the big purses to draw the big names. It seemed like a vicious circle with a furious bidding war for drivers.

DuHamel Tries Cross-Country

DuHamel was learning the hard way that the equipment had to hold together in order to take even the best driver to the chequered flag. No amount of daring, no matter how easy he could make it look, could keep a broken sled running.

The Winnipeg to St. Paul International 500 Cross Country Race was on the Polaris list of challenges, so the Can-Am team set off for Winnipeg to compete against the other factories on Ski-Doo's behalf. The cross-country racers glanced over DuHamel without much of a worry. Six hundred miles took a lot more than the 15 minutes an oval driver was used to. Cross-country racing not only took a different style of riding, it meant a different kind of snowmobile set-up and race strategy.

It certainly didn't sound like the kind of racing Yvon

DuHamel had been training for — but DuHamel was ready to try anything once. And he wasn't the only contender with something to prove. Dorothy Mercer, a 29-year-old championship skier, rodeo bronc rider, and motorcycle jockey was back for a run at the men's classes. She had already set and re-set the women's world snowmobile speed record and was ready to give the guys a run for their money.

The first couple of hundred miles of the road were flat as a pancake, one without even blueberries to create the tiniest lump. An overpass was cause for excitement, something different on the horizon.

The wind could knock winter visibility to zero in an instant. It took only five snowflakes and a light gust to pick them up to hide everything from view.

But the biggest challenge, from a rider's point of view, was the effect the wind had on the snowbanks. There is no soft powder on the prairies. Even when snow falls freshly from the sky, it's likely to lose that goose-down quality the instant the wind hurls it at a fence post and before it ever hits the ground. Ditches are full of white cement, sculpted in swirls and twirls. Even a 400-pound snowmobile, with a 200-pound driver in his gear, tearing across the bank at over 62 miles (100 km) per hour, isn't likely to leave much of a mark on it, much less dent it.

Yvon DuHamel Sets More Records

Regardless of the type of suspension the snowmobile has, it's plain rough to be a ditch rider, and that's what a lot of the Winnipeg to Minneapolis race was. Each landing connects a rider's tailbone with the frozen lump of foam that passes for a seat. If the riders are lucky, their chins stays above the handlebars, instead of pushing forward and into them.

Riding on this kind of snow, the riders don't hang on with their arms unless they're Superman. They use their legs, riding each snowdrift like it's a rodeo bronc. Luckily, by the time the eight seconds are up, the riders have moved onto another bank with a different kind of buck.

Indeed, the competition was right. What possible hope could Yvon DuHamel, professional racetrack driver, possibly have when he hit the real world of snowbanks with his snowmobile? Apparently, very little.

When the drivers lined up at the starting line, the odds were on everybody but DuHamel and Dorothy Mercer. But the first day out, 137 sleds and drivers broke before they pulled into the stop at Crookston. Leroy Lindblad, the favourite, was out. By day two, Jim Bernat was done, and Bob Eastman went on the third. By St. Cloud, Minnesota, Mercer was up to sixth in the race — and DuHamel was just ahead of her.

DuHamel faced quite a few challenges along the

way, besides adapting to the terrain. Driving a Blizzard 400, he kept the speed down around 65 miles (105 km) per hour, no matter how tempted he was to put the throttle down. At full speed it could have easily flown along at 85 miles (137 km) per hour, with his weight on it. But, he knew that the greater speed was likely to cause mechanical failure of one part or another. As it was, he had problems with a faulty clutch and a bent track sprocket. A couple of times he had to work his way through the field of drivers, to make back time lost from wrong turns.

Dorothy "Merc" Mercer, crashed during the first day, not far out of Winnipeg. Picking herself up, she climbed right back onto the sled and roared on. The next day she tangled with a barbed wire fence and had to cut herself free. It was, unfortunately, one of the hazards of cross-country driving. Then, like a few other drivers, she ran out of gas, flipped a few more times, got up, and kept on going.

Nose-dives inevitably earns the driver the title of "snowflake inspector." Likely she learned the number-one rule of coming off your sled — keep your elbows and head up off the ground, and slide on your backside to protect your clothes. That's why the seats of racers' snowmobile suits always look scuffed and worn long before the fronts do. It's not because they sit a lot...

A crowd waited at the finish line in St. Paul — the favourites had all been eliminated except for Wes Pesek, so they weren't sure what to expect as the countdown to the finish neared. Dorothy Mercer was the first to drive her Polaris past the chequered flags! She set the fastest time of the day and broke the record for the final leg, but was only third in overall time. Her cross-country record time still stands today for women.

Yvon DuHamel came up with the winning time to earn the cross-country title on his debut race. It was the first and only time Ski-Doo ever won the Winnipeg race. DuHamel was also the only driver to win a world-championship oval race, along with a prestigious cross-country title.

Speed, More Speed

In the early 1970s speed was the ultimate goal for all types of transportation. Muscle cars filled the lots at car dealers. Snowmobiles were in the big *honker* era of engines. But more than that, everybody wanted to set a bona fide record they could advertise.

The United States Snowmobile Association (USSA) stepped in to decide who had a speed record and what it was. Discarding all previous claims to a record, they set up the first formally sanctioned speed trials at Boonville, New York, on February 11, 1972.

USSA officials set up the rules and criteria to govern the event so that the results wouldn't be disputable. Each machine had to make two runs past the official timing lights on the course — with the average of the two runs being the official time. They set up a variety of classes for different engine sizes, including an unlimited class. The entries had to be snowmobiles of some sort — machines not adhering to the basic mechanical principles were disqualified.

Ski-Doo had two entries: the Inferno and the Ski-Doo X-2R. The Inferno was a rail-type dragster that promptly blew a track. The X-2R was an oversized Blizzard snowmobile powered by twin Rotax 766cc engines and piloted by Yvon DuHamel.

DuHamel, clothed in his flameproof suit, climbed onto the seat of the rumbling sled, ready to hit the trigger for his first run. The sled shot forward. It passed the timing lights at 129.2 miles (207.9 km) per hour! His return run was clocked at 125.4 (201.8 km), for an average run of 127.3 miles (204.87 km) per hour.

As the day wore on, dozens and dozens of racers roared past the timing lights. But none was able to beat DuHamel's time. Yvon DuHamel had set a snowmobile speed record that would stand for five years as a Guinness world record, until Donald J. Pitzen broke it with a speed of 135.93 miles (218.76 km) per hour on

Union Lake in Michigan, February 3, 1977.
The 1972–73 racing season brought more changes for Yvon DuHamel. The short-lived Can-Am team was dissolved, and he and Gaston Ferland were back officially as the Ski-Doo factory team. Ski-Doo brought out a truck with its name and full team support. They also hired another driver, two-time defending world champion Mike Trapp.

Other manufacturers were up in arms over Trapp joining the company. Ski-Doo's money, they claimed, had bought the 'pole' position at the world championship, making it the longstanding argument of fair racing versus bank account. Not so, claimed Bombardier and Trapp — Trapp had approached Ski-Doo looking for a full-season ride, not the half-season until January, when Yamaha withdrew its racing funds.

Trapp's forthright move brought changes to snowmobile racing teams that were much more common in other sports. Drivers sought the best ride they could get, so lots of teams changed. Factories offered almost two million dollars in contingency money to independents who won on their machines. As racers did the calculations, they realized that some of the dollars were pretty safe. In order for Sno-Jet to have to spend every bit of the one million dollars it offered, a Sno-Jet would have to win every class at every race on the approved schedule posted by the company.

As usual, Yvon DuHamel didn't start out as well as he'd have hoped. A crash when his ski broke in Peterborough took him out of the Kawartha Cup and put him flat on his back for the awards banquet. Luckily, he recovered quickly. Mike Trapp, his teammate, was still limping with a plastic cast covering a severe bruise on his leg, that he'd acquired at Mosport, Ontario, when it was time for the mid-January world championship in Eagle River.

Eagle River looked like a tough place to be for DuHamel. It had been three years since he'd earned the world championship, and the previous two had been won by his new teammate, Mike Trapp. Yamaha, who Mike had been racing with, was anxious to see the title stay with their own brand, so they had his cousins, Lynn and Wayne, out to win.

For the first time in the 10-year history of the Eagle River Derby the temperature soared and the track began to melt. Everything but the oval events were cancelled, and the promoters rushed around frantically trying to figure out how to preserve the racetrack. As a last-ditch attempt, they spread sawdust, which was readily available, over the ice surface to block the sun's rays. When the temperature thankfully dropped for the weekend, they found the new mix to be superior — it even helped prevent snow dust during the racing. Future tracks would benefit from the warm spell.

Once again, DuHamel suffered mechanical break-down, and a blown belt took his chances of recapturing the title of world champion. Both of his teammates, however, made it to the starting line for Ski-Doo. Twenty-five thousand people piled up along the banks to watch the 10th running of snowmobile racing's biggest event.

It wasn't, however, three times lucky for Mike Trapp and Ski-Doo either. Bob Eastman beat him to the che-quered flag to earn the first world championship for Polaris. Mike drove to second place.

By the end of the 1972–73 season, 315,000 brand new snowmobiles of every brand sat unsold in ware-houses. After the mild winter, the industry was way ahead of the demand. The USSA was trying to sort out the racing schedule for the sake of the manufacturers' marketing, making rules to suit everybody — but it was tough. In March of 1973, manufacturers voted 14–0 for a new pro-mod circuit. Bombardier's Ski-Doo racing director, Conrad Bernier, suggested the concept be named SnoPro. The first race was scheduled for December of 1973.

Bombardier had lots of reasons to celebrate during the summer of 1973. It's one-millionth snowmobile, a

440cc TNT Everest, rolled off the assembly line in August. Parties were in order!

However, by November the whole world was facing a fuel crisis. Bombardier met with other industry leaders to discuss cooperation in dropping all racing plans, including SnoPro. But they were met with resistance — plans were already made, money already spent. Plus, there were potentially negative implications for such drastic measures. Would the sport of snowmobiling die as quickly as it had begun? In a compromise, the USSA and other racing associations cut the length of their races in half as a fuel-conservation measure. Hundreds, perhaps thousands, did abandon the sport, but others carried on.

DuHamel's career was winding down. After three hectic years of full-time racing between snowmobile and Grand Prix Motorcycle circuits, times were changing. DuHamel's family was growing, so were his business interests in Quebec. A tremendous motorcycle crash at Talladega in late 1973 inspired a lot of rumours that he was ready to retire.

Ski-Doo, adamant about being a responsible global citizen, withdrew from racing for the 1973–74 season. Instead of sending their team to the track, they sent DuHamel and Trapp around the country, working on their Community Action Plan. DuHamel, spent the year appearing at dealerships, doing some TV, radio, newspaper, and trail riding on weekends with snowmobile clubs, to increase the profile of Ski-Doo among the people who were beginning to matter the most — the trail riders. When the Ski-Doo team returned to SnoPro for the 1974–75 season, DuHamel found some success, but the year away had taken its toll. In early January 1976, his new teammate, Larry Rugland, won the Kawartha Cup in Peterborough for the second year in a row. DuHamel's machine crashed into the board fence in an early morning accident. Both of his legs were injured. Although there was no official announcement of his retirement, after returning to Quebec to heal and tend to business, DuHamel never raced snowmobiles professionally again. His light, which shone brightly in the new sport of snowmobile racing, was soon replaced by a new constellation of stars.

Chapter 6
Gilles and Jacques Villeneuve

Gilles Villeneuve and younger brother, Jacques, were the only children of Seville and Georgette Villeneuve. Three years apart, the brothers shared similar outlooks on life and a passion for speed. The Villeneuve men were the first family of Canadian racing. Perhaps there is a racing gene in their makeup, since Gilles Villeneuve's son, Jacques, has also gone on to race Formula One cars. Or perhaps it was the French Canadian upbringing that had already produced J.-Armand Bombardier and Yvon DuHamel. Or maybe it was just a love of speed and that strong competitive instinct to be first.

Young Gilles

Little Gilles, like lots of boys, enjoyed playing with anything that was mechanical, although he was more attentive to detail than most. If his bulldozer didn't have the right number of wheels or parts he wasn't interested. The same with his trucks. He created a world of miniature roads and bridges in his sandbox, a world little brother Jacques shared.

Gilles was quietly determined, and he always challenged himself. Seeing other children riding two-wheeled bicycles without training wheels, he asked his father to remove the ones on his bicycle. Of course, the bike fell before his short legs could stop it. A few spills more and Gilles had mastered the skill. This was the pattern his life followed — first the challenge, then the fall that made him more determined, then mastery.

On weekends he had fun with his family and friends in the little community of Berthierville. He bicycled in the summer and played hockey on the frozen river in the winter. Winters were his favourite time; in fact, he declared he loved the challenge of making his way through raging blizzards, a skill that proved to be key on a snowmobile racetrack.

Before the boys could see over the car's dash, Seville held them in his lap to let them drive the car. Gilles loved to hear his father squeal the tires and pass other cars. Seville, whose first career was travelling all over the province of Quebec, tuning pianos, was a fast driver himself and often in a rush.

By 10, Gilles had a 10-speed bicycle and by 11, his father turned him loose in a nearby field with the family's battered old pick-up truck. Gilles, like J.-Armand Bombardier, also built his own mechanical toys — in fact the family lawnmower ended up as a go-cart. When Gilles was 15, his father gave him a decrepit red, 1958 MGA two-seater car. Managing to make the car run again, he performed practice runs down the lane and on an abandoned section of road.

But the practice just made Gilles want more speed. He and a friend commandeered the family's 1966 Pontiac Grand Parisienne for a secret midnight ride in a rainstorm. The car, Gilles soon discovered, went 174 kilometres per hour. Unfortunately, Gilles lost control of the car, skidded in the rain, and wrapped the Parisienne around a telephone pole. Always taught to be honest, Gilles confessed his crime. The family was left with a $4,000 loan to repay and no vehicle to show for it. That was sufficient punishment for Gilles.

The next year Gilles found himself legally driving and the proud owner of a little black MGA. While racing another sports car, a Roadrunner, both drivers encountered a herd of cows. This time Gilles had a wild rollover ride through the ditch, which resulted in 80 stitches to his scalp and no car again. With a girlfriend in the next town, Gilles moved up to a 1967 Mustang for fun. He took the road's twisting turns at less than a mile a minute, sometimes getting the 15 miles (24 km) down as low as a nine-minute trip. One thing was certain — Gilles was happiest when he had the pedal to the metal, so a racetrack was the best thing he could hope for.

With the growing popularity of snowmobiles, Gilles' father bought a Moto-Ski machine. Of course, Gilles was immediately interested. He convinced his father to let him race the orange sled at nearby events. With his mechanical skills and his love of speed, he soon brought home some trophies. A family friend, Gilles Ferland, who sold Skiroule snowmobiles, gave Gilles a modified production sled to race when he was 18 years old. Gilles won. Ferland sold snowmobiles. Everybody was happy.

That summer, in 1969, was the year Bombardier held their team trials in Valcourt. Gilles, barely 18 years old, was missed in the review. Had he joined Yvon DuHamel as a teammate, the snowmobile industry would have had a very different history. Paired with the older French Canadian as a mentor, who had years of experience racing motorcycles under his belt, Gilles' genius for driving and mechanics would likely have driven the evolution of Ski-Doo even faster. Instead, as it was, Gilles fought his way up through the ranks of minor manufacturers on tight or almost non-existent budgets, producing innovations that eventually worked their way through the system.

The next winter, in 1969–70, Gilles Villeneuve was hired by the Skiroule factory, as a driver/mechanic. Having finished school, Gilles was happy to land a job doing what he loved best. Joann Barthe, his steady girl-friend, often went with him to races. Life was good.

But things rarely go as planned. Gilles and Joann, expecting their first child, decided to get married in October 1970. Skiroule notified Gilles that he was no longer needed as a driver. He'd done well for the com-pany — perhaps too well. He refused to stay north of the border racing, since the biggest money was in the United States. With two parts of the company, Canadian and U.S., the racing department wanted things a certain way. Gilles knew his skills and refused to give up the higher-paying U.S. racing events for company policy, so they parted company.

Gilles went shopping for a sponsor and landed Moto-Ski. They gave him three machines, technical assistance, and some expense money, which, although he wasn't considered part of a factory team, at least pro-vided some private team support.

Racing to put groceries on the table, Gilles was aggressive throughout Quebec. While his own expenses were mostly covered, he had a wife and home to think about. He won the Quebec championship in his class, as well as the 440cc World Series title in New York to end the season in style. Then, on April 9, 1971, he became the proud father of Jacques, who he named for his brother.

Gilles bought a mobile home for his family and parked it across from his parents' property; then he bought himself a school bus he named Big Bertha. He equipped part of Bertha as his living quarters, the other part as a shop and trailer. Ready for the 1971–72 season, he found he had to go shopping for another ride.

Moto-Ski, manufactured by Les Industries Bouchard in La Pocatiére, Quebec, had an excellent snowmobile. In fact, it was so good that it was stiff competition for Bombardier's Ski-Doos in Valcourt. In a business decision that expanded their product line and acquired a needed factory, Bombardier purchased Moto-Ski in 1971. The deal, of course, left young Gilles without a sponsor, since Ski-Doo didn't have team trials that year for their team.

Once again, history or perhaps destiny played against Gilles. If Ski-Doo had run team trials, there's little doubt that Gilles would have been invited since he was already involved with Moto-Ski, their new line.

There's also no doubt he would have earned a place on the team, making his life over the next few years much less a challenge than it was to be. However, Gilles worked harder without factory mechanics and support to modify the machines he did ride. Without wins, his family didn't eat, so Gilles did everything in his power to make those wins.

That winter, Gilles rode the big, red Alouettes to victory throughout the province. With 14 races, he spent a lot of time on the road. His wife struggled through the snowbanks at home, lugging baby Jacques in and out of the trailer. Learning how to thaw frozen pipes and fix overworked heating systems, Joann Villeneuve made the best of things.

Ending another great season, Gilles had 10 championships. The four races he didn't win had all been due to mechanical failure, similar to the experiences of Yvon DuHamel. Gilles began to rely on his own mechanical skills, spending lots of time trying to improve the fragile rubber-belt drive system that blew up his chances of winning at some of the races.

The next winter he travelled further afield, taking his Alouette across the border to the more lucrative races. He earned about $5,000 that winter and finished as overall Canadian snowmobile champion. In July 1973, his daughter, Melanie, was born.

All the winning made Gilles anxious to add summer racing to his schedule. He went to the Jim Russell driving school at Le Circuit Mont Tremblant. On the first drive, he shot out past his classmates, proving his expertise, and was granted a racing license. Big Bertha went out for the summer and Gilles won 7 of 10 races with a two-year-old car he'd purchased. Plus, he was Rookie of the Year and the Formula Ford Champion for Quebec. Gilles Villeneuve was hooked with racing fever.

Jacques Joins the Team
After a great first season, Alouette had confidence in Gilles. Plus, his successes on the car track didn't hurt his reputation with the Quebec manufacturer. There was a good budget for the young Villeneuve, whose name was known by every snowmobiler across the province.

In the fall of 1973, Gilles Villeneuve brought along his younger brother, Jacques, as an additional mechanic and driver for Alouette. He also brought a series of designs, fresh off of his drafting board, to apply to the sleds. His ideas included an innovative wishbone suspension similar to those he'd seen on racecars, but there were lots of kinks to be worked out in the design.

Big Bertha was on the road again, this time taking the Villeneuve brothers across the border. In only three months they'd built Gilles' newly designed twin-track snowmobile with its fancy new suspension. Working together like a team who shared one another's thoughts, Gilles and Jacques Villeneuve were ready to hit the big time and the brand-new professional snowmobile racing SnoPro season.

On Monday, December 3, 1973, the first SnoPro race, which was scheduled for Ironwood, Michigan, was cancelled — not due to the world fuel crisis either. The reason was, no snow. The promoters, however, were also nervous about how many spectators would show up with all the controversy about burning fuel for sport. The next day a blizzard hit Ironwood. The race was quickly revived.

Entries poured in. Stock machines, driven by amateur or non-factory drivers, enjoyed the even field of competition. Friday and Saturday proved to be great with the new SnoPro arrangement, although the crowd waited in anticipation for the big boys to come out to play on Sunday.

By 7 a.m. on Sunday morning the grandstands in the Gogebic County Fairgrounds were already half full. Back in Big Bertha, the Villeneuve brothers were frantically wrenching on the Alouette, and had been most of the night. Observers noticed the telltale flicker of blue welding much earlier, at 4:30 a.m.

The crowd, anxious for the first sight of the all-powerful new sleds the factories had been building for SnoPro, was somewhat disappointed, well, at least until the Alouette roared out. It was bright red — a real show-stopper. Longer than other snowmobiles, it stretched a full three metres from hood to tail flap. It looked, not like a snowmobile, but like a futuristic flying machine, with its bullet shape and enclosed body. And they couldn't even see the biggest innovation of all, the twin tracks under the enclosed shape.

Other mechanics and racers in the pits were also attracted to the Alouette. It was new. It was innovative. But would it work?

Ironwood's snow, not even a week old, hadn't had a chance to pack up yet. After two days of stock machines roaring around, there were problems. When the SnoPro machines started flying over it at 90-plus miles (145 km) per hour, a mean hole opened up in turn two. The Alouette's twin tracks didn't have a chance — they derailed. Despite making it to all three finals and prov-ing the cornering abilities of the new design, the Villeneuve brothers didn't take home the money.

The Villeneuves rushed back to Canada to do some more wrenching. Gilles abandoned the motorcycle-style transmission, with its six speeds, and switched back to more traditional chain case components. Ready to try again, Big Bertha rolled into Peterborough, Ontario.

A large crowd of 30,000 Canadians gathered to cheer for the innovative new Alouette on January 6, 1973. It was a momentous day for the new design. Starting at the back of the 440cc pack, Gilles worked his way through the field. By the fourth lap, he caught the leader, Dave Thompson, on his Arctic Cat. He was cautious in the next six laps, his goal just to keep in front. His strategy worked — on its second time out the new Alouette won its SnoPro class.

The 1974 World Championship

Like Yvon DuHamel before him and numerous drivers still to come, the first big win with the twin tracker just whet Gilles' appetite for more. And, of course, winning the world championship on the Alouette was just too fragile a dream to be spoken out loud.

The 1974 Eagle River World Championship Derby featured a new half-mile oval track to go along with the new SnoPro class. The fuel shortage hadn't been as dramatic as everyone feared, so while there were cutbacks, life went on.

Nineteen seventy-four was Gilles Villeneuve's second trip to the world championship, although he hadn't made it into the finals the year before. Gilles had a game plan ready that required lots of work. All of the Alouettes were drilled out and stripped down to the bare minimum to make them as light as possible. The plan was to run the twin-tracker in the Modified class, then switch things back to run the 650cc three-cylinder for Sunday afternoon. Even though the SnoPro organization was running the event, the feature world-championship race ran under Eagle River's own rules, not those of the racing organization.

It was another warm year for the Derby. Highways were iced over with rain and sleet. Big Bertha, however, ploughed through. So did other drivers. The weekend's entries totalled a new high, just over 600. Spectators, no doubt enjoying the pleasant temperatures, also flocked to the track in high numbers. However, since it continued to drizzle on and off through the entire event, it ended up being one of the least comfortable on record.

The design of the new Eagle River racetrack didn't favour the handling of the Alouette twin-tracker. Gilles took it out for two SnoPro heats, then set about making modifications to the other sleds in his fleet, since the twin-tracker kept derailing on the tight corners. He'd applied his new technology to all of his Alouettes, so they had open chain cases, with gears held in place by quick-release pins. Between heats, the brothers wrenched madly, sliding gears, chain case and all, off the sleds and replacing them with ones in a different ratio. Finally, they were happy — the acceleration and top speed matched the track exactly. Although they hadn't scored in the big SnoPro classes of the weekend, Gilles made it through the eliminations with his three-cylinder 650cc racer for his chance at the world championship.

It was Sunday afternoon in Eagle River. The mist, originally just a mild inconvenience for spectators, turned into a steady rain. Twenty thousand spectators, however, lined the hill at Eagle River, their attention focused on the world-championship race.

There had been some major changes to Eagle River's track, modernizing it to the form it has today. Rather than the steeply banked track Yvon DuHamel and his competitors had raced around a brief four years earlier, the new Eagle River half-mile oval track was nearly flat. There were new viewing platforms in the corners, and a press tower. Double fencing provided more protection for spectators, reflecting the whole industry movement on safety issues.

Gilles started his Alouette in the pits, then made his way onto the track. Jacques put down his wrenches, ready to watch the main event of the weekend.

The field was strong. There were three Polaris drivers, four Arctic Cat, and two Yamahas. Ski-Doo, of course, was absent as DuHamel was visiting dealerships and doing trail rides for Ski-Doo, instead of racing. And then, there was the one lone Alouette in the rapidly shrinking field of highly competitive snowmobile manufacturers. The lone Canadian, representing the lone Canadian snowmobile manufacturer at the race, Gilles Villeneuve was ready to win.

If fate had prevented Gilles from linking his future with Ski-Doo, this was the moment at stake.

The engines roared as the drivers found their place in the line-up at the start line. Trail snowmobiles of the time rated around 106 dBA (decibels) at the driver's ear, while race sleds rated higher. Modern ratings class 80 dBA as a hazardous level, with levels of 120 dBA downright painful. Ten drivers faced the race director. Nine of them were fully decked in the newest innovation — racing leathers. SnoPro was about looking like you were the top dog on the block, after all, so each team wore specially designed leather snowmobile suits, consisting of jackets and bib-front pants, to match their sleds. Leather gave the drivers by far the best range of mobility and comfort of any material.

Under the white bib number 3469, with its Quebec flag emblazoned in the top left-hand corner, Gilles wore a ski jacket, it's hood lined with the common creamy white lining of the time that resembled sheep's wool, and knitted cuffs above his gloves.

The race director stood in front of the 10 drivers.

Gilles was in the pole position, while Larry Coltom had the outside line.

Gilles Villeneuve gave his ready nod, then gazed out over his sled. In front of him, the three big cylinders stuck through the hood like ornaments. The throttle cables, also hanging out in the open, joined from all three carbs into a single line that fed through the handlebars to the throttle lever. Like the rest of the sled, even the bar was modified — a metal rod, barely 30 centimetres long, with the standard racing hoops curved into the ends.

The rest of the drivers, fingers poised over the throttle, also gave the ready nod.

The green flag waved.

Gilles hit the trigger and was off.

Coltom led through the first corner. Gilles Villeneuve was having trouble with the sled — it was only running on two cylinders! Once the third one kicked in, the race rapidly changed, with Gilles charging to the front of the pack. Nobody could catch him. After the first five laps, Gilles started to take it easy on his belt — a blow-up would take his win away faster than the drivers behind him on the track.

The crowd cheered, although they didn't know the name of the driver on the bright red sled. Even the announcer on the PA system couldn't quite figure out who was leading the race. But from the moment the 1974 world-championship race ended, the name of Gilles Villeneuve continued to spread in racing circles around the world.

Gilles picked up the chequered flag to make his victory lap.

The first to extend his congratulations to the unknown driver was Bob Eastman, defending champion of the title, as Villeneuve slowed to a halt at the end of his lap.

The young French Canadian, only the second Canadian to win the Eagle River World Championship, took home the title for the small Quebec company, Alouette. But there was much more to come for the Villeneuves.

Chapter 7
Racing Triumps

hen Gilles Villeneuve ran away with his world-championship title for Alouette in 1974, there was still lots of racing left in the year. Joann Villeneuve, Gilles' wife, had left the children at home with grandparents and travelled along to Eagle River to watch his win. She was thrilled for her husband's success and for the healthy paychecks he collected with his wins.

The Season Draws to a Close

Jacques Villeneuve, however, was also starting to pull in some pretty good paychecks. In February, rather than going with his brother Gilles to the SnoPro race in New

York, he headed to Beausejour, Manitoba, for the Canadian Power Toboggan Championships (CPTC). The year before, Gilles had won 9 of the 10 classes he entered, and Jacques was determined to hold up the family tradition.

The Canadian Power Toboggan Championships had a tradition older than Eagle River's, so organizers knew how to put on a great race. The crowd was happy to welcome another Villeneuve to town — and the good times rolled.

Through the week Jacques won the 340, 440, and 650 Modified classes. His paycheck totalled $3,150! Better yet, he didn't disappoint big brother Gilles by losing with the Alouette they'd worked so hard to build.

For the first time ever, Eagle River was also hosting a race other than their own world's championship. The USSA held the fifth annual World Series there the last weekend in February. With all the January rains, the ice was keen and the track was fast. The number of drivers was bigger at the race than it ever would be again.

This time it was Jacques Villeneuve's turn to shine on the unique Eagle River track. The fans were waiting for Mod III, where Jacques' beautiful red Alouette would run against Mike Lauter's short, squat Arctic Cat. Which style would win? Jacques led through the race, with Lauter working his way up from the back of the pack.

Jacques drove his usual smooth line.

Going into the sharp corners he back-steered the sled, throwing his slight body over the inside edge until he nearly touched the ice, to keep the sled on the ice. Each corner was more graceful than the one before as he gained experience on the daunting track.

The white flag dropped. One lap left.

At turn three, Lauter drew up beside him. It was a drag race to the chequered flag and victory, but Jacques Villeneuve took second.

The next race, however, had a different result. Jumping onto his Mod IV machine, Jacques pulled onto the icy track, which was covered with nearly three centimetres of loose corn snow. It was late in the day, almost dusk. Developing the style he'd soon become famous for, Jacques slid through the corners to victory.

As the 1974 season ended, brother Gilles Villeneuve placed in the top 10 SnoPro drivers, despite having made only five races. That was cause for elation!

However, there was also bad news for the Villeneuve brothers. The Alouette snowmobile company went into receivership in Quebec. After all the work they'd put into the sleds, the brothers announced plans to buy the company's racers and continue as independents.

Back home, for Gilles' wife, Joann, there was even more news. Gilles had sold their mobile home to buy a racecar. She went to bed with a migraine for six weeks, then joined him with the children in the little camper atop the pick-up truck.

When Quebec's maple trees donned their fall colours in 1974, the Villeneuve brothers were in anything but cheerful spirits. Gilles' home was gone. His leg, which he'd broken during a car race at Mosport, Ontario, still hurt. He had $20,000 in assorted debts. And, of course with Alouette bankrupt, they had no sponsor for the upcoming snowmobile season.

The brothers had learned the one solemn truth in racing — *there is no tomorrow*. Rides could disappear as fast as they appeared. Money fell through their fingers racing. It didn't matter how much they won, there was always somewhere else to spend it.

They were determined to make their future. Putting the Alouettes back into service, along with Big Bertha, they hit the Canadian circuits to regain lost fortunes, or at least keep going. The economics of self-sponsored racing meant they had to make as few miles as possible.

But Eagle River's 1975 world championship was slotted in, regardless of cost. Ski-Doo was back that year; however, the drivers were scrambling to catch up after a lost year. Politics were playing havoc with the SnoPro events — there was a Professional Drivers

Circuit, along with the factory drivers.

With the Alouette a year behind in technology, Gilles Villeneuve was in a poor position to defend his title. The competition was newer, faster, and had more money behind it. The final field for the world championship included three factory Polaris sleds, one Arctic Cat, one Rupp, one reconstructed Polaris, two Mercuries, and Gilles on his Alouette.

Gilles wasn't in the race long. Half-blinded by heavy snow dust neither the crowd nor the drivers could tell what colour the machines were, Gilles soon slowed to a stop. Mechanical failure cost him the race.

After a so-so season, Gilles Villeneuve headed for the cars once again when the ice melted. He became manager, mechanic, racer, and even truck driver. Working frantically to get his car ready for the first race, he drove 53 hours straight to arrive in Edmonton for the practice.

Peter Hill, marketing manager and vice-president of Skiroule admired the determination the young French Canadian exhibited on the track. In the summer of 1975 he negotiated a racing deal with the Villeneuve brothers that provided some car sponsorship and gave them Skiroule factory support for snowmobiling. By the end of the Formula Atlantic car-racing season, Gilles Villeneuve finished in fifth place.

When fall rolled around, it was round-the-clock work on the new Skiroule sleds. Unlike his first year with the Skiroule factory, Gilles was in charge this time. He'd not only learned numerous things from his twin-tracked Alouette, he also understood a lot about racing cars. Drawing from all of his expertise and applying his creative thinking, he built another line of innovative racing machines.

The new Skiroules, unlike the big SnoPro Alouette, were sleek and tiny. They fit him and brother Jacques like gloves. Taking his innovations even further this time, the sleds had seats built for the left-turn position. As well, he created the little, pointed, alloy skis that soon became popular.

But, as usual, there was more work to be done than even the two dedicated Villeneuve brothers could accomplish. In previous years, the sight of them sleeping on an empty bench near the sleds had already become a common enough sight. The little green machines weren't ready until the big January race at Peterborough — even then, the last screws were tightened in the hotel garage.

It was 1976, and Peterborough's Kawartha Cup was once again up for grabs. Gilles Villeneuve, of course, hoped to take the Canadian championship. Things looked promising too. The machines sounded strong and the practice laps were good. Then, in the first heat race, Gilles shocked everyone and took the chequered flag. But the good luck wasn't to continue. Neither of the Villeneuve brothers came out winners that weekend.

It was at this Peterborough race that Yvon DuHamel had his last race for Ski-Doo. The Villeneuve brothers were emerging as the biggest names on the Canadian snowmobile tracks. Due to Skiroule's marketing goals, the new green machines were supposed to focus on Canadian races and Canadian wins, rather than hitting the U.S. circuits. The company, struggling against strong competition, needed to do everything it could to hope for survival.

Gilles did, however, manage to make it to the 12th International Grand Prix Kilkenny Cup races at Lancaster, New Hampshire, on January 24–25. It was a weekend the racing world would remember, as the green machines cleaned up all the SuperMod classes on Saturday and Sunday. The independent new front-end design on the little Skiroules were the envy of all the other racers on the rough track. Gilles Villeneuve's innovations kept his sled running smooth and fast.

The next weekend, Jacques Villeneuve was the one who startled his American competition by snatching the SuperMod 250 from Arctic Cat. It was Skiroule's first major SnoPro victory, and took place at Bangor, Maine.

Racing Triumphs

Back in Quebec, the big SnoPro teams rolled in for two big events on the weekend of February 7–8. Gilles was in fine form with the little Skiroule, fairly flying around the track. He won six of the eight SnoPro events at Quebec City on Saturday and Montreal on Sunday. The Villeneuve Skiroule racing team had the attention of the racing world.

While the idea for the Villeneuves' independent front suspension had been around for a while, it hadn't exactly been a success. Gilles had even tried it on his Alouettes. The modifications he made to the Skiroule that season, however, were about to revolutionize not only snowmobile racing, but soon, trail riding. The year ended as a success that would be measured more in the years to come than by what the Villeneuve brothers were able to put in the bank.

The car-racing season during the summer of 1976 proved to be the one that made Gilles' career. He wrapped up the championship well before the end of the season — showing a clear dominance in North American F-A racing. An invitation from Teddy Mayer of Team McLaren for test driving was about to launch him into the world arena. In the spring of 1977 his Formula One career would begin. When McLaren let him go after one ride, Ferrari quickly signed him — it was his only team change in Formula One, after eight years of looking for a snowmobile ride.

Meanwhile, Jacques had started his own career in auto racing. He earned the 1976 Honda Civic Championship Rookie of the Year award for his first season. By the 1977 season he won the Honda Civic Championship Champion of the Year in all categories.

Between car racing seasons, Jacques Villeneuve was left to deal with problems at Skiroule. Due, they said, to a series of complex problems, the Canadian manufacturer withdrew from SnoPro. Once again, Jacques was looking for a winter ride.

The Winter of 1976–77

On his own, without either a racing partner or a sponsor, Jacques Villeneuve was quickly recruited by Gary Mathers of Kawasaki. Kawasaki was sponsoring its first, and only, professional oval-track racing team for the 1976–77 winter season.

Jacques was a valuable asset to the team because of his experience with the coil-spring suspensions that Kawasaki, along with other manufacturers, had just started working with. But the Kawasaki team faced bigger problems than new technology. SnoPro rules stipulated that the machines run in the SnoPro classes had to be based on production crankcases from their consumer sleds. This was a big disadvantage for

Kawasaki since their current run of power plants weren't designed for the type of output required to be competitive on the professional circuits.

While Kawasaki did a great job of building light, easily handled sleds, the drivers couldn't overcome the lack of power. Jacques made a good showing across the country but didn't end up in the prizes.

That year there was lots of snow in Beausejour, Manitoba, and it was cold. New fans were materializing everywhere, ready to brave all the elements to see the big boys race their sleds in the SnoPro classes. The racing program for the year advertised the events as "The Greatest Show on Earth."

In order to sponsor a professional show, local organizations were required to put up at least $10,000 in prize money for a two-day event. A USSA crew was hand-picked to follow the SnoPro drivers and to man the key stations, like race director. Of course, that meant a consistent application of the rules with a USSA technical director, pit marshal, and chief scorer — more often referred to as the race secretary.

The February 25–26, 1977, Beausejour event followed the first SnoPro race in Saskatchewan, at Waldheim, in the northern part of the province. Rather than returning to the east or stateside, drivers took a leisurely trip down to begin testing on Beausejour's track and tuning their sleds in their well-equipped semi-trailers.

It was a big weekend of events, since the races were integrated into the annual Farewell to Winter festival. Before the official opening of the races at noon on Saturday, spectators gathered to watch the Mayor's Challenge Snowshoe Race at the Beausejour Brokenhead Centre, which was at the racetrack.

With all their years of experience running races, the Beausejour track facilities were superb. The kitchen was well stocked, offering more than the usual hot dog fare. Indeed you could have a nice fat kielbasa sausage in a bun or a bowl of steaming hot borscht with a big dollop of sour cream to warm yourself from the inside out.

With non-stop action, race day was more than a newcomer could have possibly imagined. The half-mile track was a sheet of ice so keen most curlers would have been happy to chuck rocks on it. For a five-dollar pit pass and an insurance waiver, spectators wandered through the semi-trailers in the pits, looking for their own favourite teams and drivers. They could even get an autograph if they were lucky enough to find a driver not wrenching his sled or taking off for a hot lap.

Around 4,000 fans stood in the snowbanks at the track edge to watch Saturday's racing. It was a combined North American–Canadian Championships, so the racers were pushing hard. A good start was a key factor in a win. But it didn't happen for everyone.

Once in a while a sled didn't start. The race director started his two-minute timer. At the end, the sled either had to be running or dragged to the side. Sometimes it started and the racer jumped on to give the ready nod. Sometimes it didn't, and a frustrated driver pulled it out of the way. The odd driver chucked his helmet after the machine, as if he was throwing in the towel. But of course, the flare of anger never lasted long; it was just momentary disappointment. He was always out for the next heat.

Sunday, the crowd swelled to 10,000 in the tiny community of Beausejour. It truly was a festival atmosphere. Smiles spread across faces. Toques and brightly coloured snowmobile suits showed brand support. The air was full of the sweet smell of running snowmobiles, while the whine of the engines racing down the track filled the ears of the audience.

Jacques Villeneuve didn't win any prizes that weekend, but he did drive with the flair that led to his nickname — the Flying French Canadian. Steve Decker won the Canadian Power Toboggan Championship with his Ski-Doo and lost it over a technicality, to Richmond, B.C., Yamaha team driver Larry Omans.

Independent front suspension, which the

Villeneuve brothers successfully implemented on the Alouette the previous racing season, had quickly been adopted by the designers at Polaris. In most of the classes it was indeed a weekend for Polaris fans, as their independent-front-suspension sleds made a clean sweep except for one third-place finish in the 440X class by a Ski-Doo. Polaris also cleaned house in Super-Mod I, Super-Mod II, and Super-Mod III. Beausejour's long sweeping corners were perfect for the newly designed Polaris machines.

For Jacques Villeneuve, it was the final year with small factories, since he soon went on to tie his fortunes to Ski-Doo.

The 1980 World Championship
The sunrise over Eagle River's World Championship Snowmobile Derby track on January 20, 1980, revealed as much activity as a honeybee hive in a July clover field. The *zing* of fine-tuned snowmobile engines chasing one another around the racetrack filled the air. A rich smell of burning aviation fuel mixed with snowmobile oil drifted on the early morning mists.

Jacques Villeneuve zipped up his black, yellow, and orange Ski-Doo leathers and pulled on his tight-fitting gloves. Grabbing his red Dr. Pepper cap, he jumped out of the semi-trailer to have one more talk with his mechanics.

Racing Triumphs

The pits still showed the effect of the previous week's thaw. Ice lay not in the usual sheet but in patchy blotches over the ground. Of course, the carbide runners on the skis of the powerful sleds had also done their share of damage over the weekend.

As the morning turned into afternoon, the hubbub of activity around the pit area increased. After each silence, the roar of another race beginning marked the passage of time.

One of Jacques' sponsors patted him on the back. It was a Ski-Doo weekend; Mike Decker had taken Super Stock II and III, while Chuck Decker ran away with I.

There was lots of pressure on Jacques Villeneuve to win the Eagle River World Championship this second year on the Ski-Doo factory team. It had been a full decade since Yvon DuHamel took the last world title home for Ski-Doo. And it had been six years since another Canadian, big brother Gilles Villeneuve, had won the title.

Nineteen eighty also marked the year of the first Formula One championship class of 340cc engines — the beginning of a new era.

As the time grew closer, Jacques went back into the trailer to tape up his face. Grabbing the roll of silver duct tape, he carefully tore off a strip and applied it across his nose, then, added another one. There was a little bit of a crease on the right side, but it didn't feel like any air would come through it. He added a little more tape, took a deep breath, and blew it out to make sure.

He pulled on his bright orange helmet, then worked his way through staging with his number-96 sled. The other nine drivers who qualified for the world championship, along with their teams, were doing the same thing.

Jacques pulled up at the start line and gazed out at the crowd. Twenty-four thousand race fans clustered around the fences and up the hillside, anxious for the race to begin. He took a few minutes to sit, not facing the crowd or the sled's handlebars, to concentrate and gather his thoughts.

It was 3 p.m.

Ted Otto, race director, pulled the 10 racers aside to explain exactly how the green-flag start would work.

Jacques Villeneuve yanked the recoil rope. The Ski-Doo fired and ran. Positioned on the inside of the track, he was the first to nod as Ted's flag went down the line of drivers, pointing. He was ready.

Ted stuck the end of the green flag into the ice.

With a quick flip of his wrist and his signature hop, Ted whipped the flag into the air.

Jacques hammered the trigger. He felt the smooth acceleration of the Ski-Doo under him and the tremen-

Jacques Villeneuve in his 1982 racing Ski-Doo

dous roar of the field around him. The other nine sleds were just inches away.

Into corner one...sliding...around the corner... grabbing a handful of throttle and out of the corner... Jacques pulled into the lead of the world-championship race.

At the end of lap one Jacques Villeneuve was the uncontested leader. With the next 14 laps he inched further and further ahead of the field. When he took the chequered flag of the 1980 Eagle River World Championship race, Brad Hulings, SnoPro points leader, was a third of a lap behind him on his Scorpion. Elsner, the 1979 World Champion, was that much further behind again, taking third place.

In the Victory Circle, Jacques' brother, Gilles Villeneuve, gave him a hearty handshake. It was Jacques Villeneuve's proudest moment.

Epilogue
The Legacy

J.-Armand Bombardier

Bombardier, Inc. grew to be one of Canada's largest and most important corporations. As well as producing snowmobiles, it added other lines of recreational vehicles: Sea-Doos and ATVs. With diversification over the decades, it became one of the world's largest manufacturers of aircraft, including the Learjet and railway equipment.

Bombardier remained family-owned and operated in the methods that J.-Armand Bombardier set up before his death in 1964. During 2003 the company restructured, selling some assets and stocks. However, Ski-Doo snowmobiles, Bombardier's legacy, will continue to be a part of winter around the globe.

J.-Armand Bombardier was inducted into the Canadian Business Hall of Fame (CBHF). CBHF inductees are selected by an independent selection committee, representing Canada's foremost business, academic, and media institutions.

In 1994, Bombardier was inducted into the

International Snowmobile Hall of Fame. He was recognized as a pioneer in snowmobile design, innovation, and manufacture. He is acknowledged as the creator and manufacturer of the first rider-over-tunnel snowmobile.

In 1989, Bombardier was inducted into the Snowmobile Racing Hall of Fame as an inventor who contributed to the sport. He introduced and patented many of the concepts that made it possible for the vehicle to become a performance machine suitable for racing. The sprocket-driven track, the wheeled track suspension, and many more innovations were developed in Valcourt.

The Musée J.-Armand Bombardier in Valcourt, Quebec, presents the life and work of the great inventor. The privately funded exhibition also describes the evolution of the snowmobile industry, in part launched by the Quebec visionary. The Bombardier Garage, the inventor's original workshop, has been completely restored and is part of the museum.

Yvon DuHamel
Yvon DuHamel was one of the original 10 snowmobile racers inducted into the Snowmobile Racing Hall of Fame at its inception banquet in 1989. He was honoured as one of the first true racing professionals. His efforts

during the fuel crisis on behalf of Ski-Doo are remembered by snowmobile fans and racers across the country. In 1999 DuHamel was inducted into the Motorcycle Racing Hall of Fame (MRHF). The American Motorcycle Heritage Foundation was created in 1982, with its mission to establish the MRHF to honour those who have made significant contributions to all aspects of motorcycling. DuHamel's accomplishments are listed as a 1970s AMA Road Racer.

DuHamel continued motorcycle racing over the years. In 2002, he was still placing in races sponsored by the Vintage Road Racing Association, held in Mosport, Shannonville, and North Bay, Ontario, even though he was over 60 years old.

The Grand-Prix de Valcourt started in 1983 as a major winter event, although the name for the first two years was the Grand-Prix St. Laurent. Now, the track hosts races at the Yvon DuHamel Circuit. The track is near both the Bombardier manufacturing plant and the Museum in Valcourt.

Both of DuHamel's sons, Mario and Miguel, went on to race motorcycles professionally. Miguel has an impressive list of superbike wins racing for Honda America. In 1995, Miguel was the first Canadian to win the AMA Superbike title. Mario did well with the SuperTwins. The boys, they say, got their start racing mini-bikes in the basement of the family home.

Gilles Villeneuve

Gilles Villeneuve died on May 8, 1982, behind the wheel of his Ferrari, in a high-speed collision during a qualifying race for the Dutch Grand Prix at Zolder. Often described as one of the most exciting racers to take the track, Villeneuve's name is still remembered as one of the truly great Canadians more than 20 years after his death.

In the last race of the 1978 Formula One racing season, Gilles took the chequered flag for the first time. To the joy of Canadian fans, he accomplished this on home turf, at the Montreal Grand Prix. Originally known as the Circuit Ile-Notre-Dame, the track was renamed the Circuit Gilles Villeneuve by the City of Montreal just two weeks after his death in 1982.

Gilles Villeneuve's son, Jacques Villeneuve, also became a race driver, making a sensational Formula One debut in 1996. He continues to race Formula One.

Gilles Villeneuve was inducted into the Canadian Motorsports Hall of Fame and the Grand Prix Hall of Fame. There is also a Gilles Villeneuve Museum in Berthierville, Quebec, where he was raised.

As well, Gilles was one of the original 10 snowmobile racers inducted into the Snowmobile Racing Hall of

Fame at its inception banquet in 1989. They recognized not only his skills as a driver but also his mechanical genius for having built the first twin-track race sled, and the first true IFS (independent front suspension) to appear in oval competition.

Jacques Villeneuve

In 1980, when Jacques Villeneuve won his first Eagle River World Championship Snowmobile Race, he was also the Formula Atlantic (FA) car-racing champion, with four wins, including the Canadian Grand Prix.

The Flying French Canadian, as he was known, was also the FA champion in 1981. His winter was impressive too, although he missed the world championship title with the first-ever Bombardier twin-track snowmobile due to lack of a holeshot. In 1982, however, he regained the title for Ski-Doo and Canada. That year found him in second place in the Can-Am championship.

A subsequent move to Indy cars kept Jacques out of snowmobile racing for a few years, as he was too busy. He was the first Canadian to win an Indy car race. By 1986 he was back on the ice with his Ski-Doo, becoming the first driver to take the world championship for the third time. In 1987 he was the champion of the Ski-Doo sport series.

As the years rolled on Jacques continued to

dedicate more and more of his time to the sport he loved — snowmobile racing. In 2003, at the 40th running of the Eagle River World Championship Snowmobile Derby, he was still racing, even though he would soon turn 50 years old. Thirty years after his first competition there, Jacques Villeneuve made yet another victory lap. On January 19, 2003, during the Friday Night Thunder special event, Jacques won the Formula One Shootout. It was the same class that began when he captured his first world championship, 23 years earlier in 1980.

When asked why he still races, Jacques replied, "What else is there to do? I like the designing part of it. I'm not a guy that is always satisfied with something. I want to do better. My brother Gilles was the same way. Every lap is the most important."

The crowd roared in Eagle River at that race, as they do all over North America, to cheer the Flying French Canadian on.

Bibliography

Donaldson, G. *Gilles Villeneuve: The Life of the Legendary Racing Driver.* Toronto: McClelland & Stewart, 1989.

Ingham, L. Allister. *As the Snow Flies — A history of snowmobile development in North America.* Lanigan: Snowmobile Research Publishing, 2000

MacDonald, L. *The Bombardier Story: Planes, Trains, and Snowmobiles.* Toronto: John Wiley & Sons, 2002.

Ramstad, C.J. & Bob Satran. *Of Ice and Engines.* Deephaven: PPM Books, 1987.

Villeneuve, J, with Gerald Donaldson. *Villeneuve Winning in Style.* London: CollinsWinslow, 1997.

Vint, B. *Warriors of Winter.* Milwaukee: Market Communications, 1977.

About the Author

Linda Aksomitis spent a decade on racetracks throughout Canada and the United States with her husband, David, and their racing team, during the 1980s and early 1990s. Today she is a full-time writer, with travel writing one of her favourite genres. She still hits the snowmobile trails with her Ski-Doo MXZ, along with her husband on his Ski-Doo REV, enjoying the thrill of winter. Her husband is enjoying initiating their grandson, Jonathon, into the love of snowmobiling, with his Mini-Z.

Photo Credits

All photographs are reproduced courtesy of the Musée J.-Armand Bombardier, Valcourt, Québec. Special thanks are due to Guy Pépin for his help with selecting and procuring the photographs.